W9-AOT-053

Cowboys Count,
Monkeys
Measure,
and Princesses
Problem Solve

Cowboys Count, Monkeys Measure, and Princesses Problem Solve

BUILDING EARLY MATH SKILLS THROUGH STORYBOOKS

by

Jane M. Wilburne, Ed.D.

Jane B. Keat, Ph.D.

and

Mary Napoli, Ph.D.

Penn State Harrisburg

·P·A·U·L·H·
BROOKES
PUBLISHING C⁰®

Baltimore • London • Sydney

Paul H. Brookes Publishing Co.
Post Office Box 10624
Baltimore, Maryland 21285-0624
USA

www.brookespublishing.com

Typeset by Integrated Publishing Solutions, Grand Rapids, Michigan.
Manufactured in the United States of America by
Sheridan Books, Inc., Chelsea, Michigan.

Library of Congress Cataloging-in-Publication Data

Wilburne, Jane M.
  Cowboys count, monkeys measure, and princesses problem solve : building early math skills through storybooks / by Jane M. Wilburne, Ed.D., Jane B. Keat, Ph.D. and Mary Napoli, Ph.D.
    p.   cm.
  Includes bibliographical references and index.
  ISBN-13: 978-1-59857-106-6
  ISBN-10: 1-59857-106-0
  1. Mathematics--Study and teaching (Primary)—Activity programs. 2. Storytelling. I. Keat, Jane B. II. Napoli, Mary. III. Title.
  QA135.6.W55 2011
  372.7—dc22   2011006209

British Library Cataloguing in Publication data are available from the British Library.

2015   2014   2013   2012   2011

10   9   8   7   6   5   4   3   2   1

Contents

About the Authors

Jane M. Wilburne, Ed.D., Associate Professor of Mathematics Education, Penn State Harrisburg, 777 West Harrisburg Pike, W331 Olmsted Building, Middletown, Pennsylvania 17057

Dr. Wilburne teaches undergraduate and graduate courses in mathematics education. Her research interests are preservice teachers' self-efficacy with mathematical problem solving, elementary teachers' teaching of mathematical problem solving through storybooks, and teaching and assessment of higher order thinking and problem solving. She has three grown children and one granddaughter.

Jane B. Keat, Ph.D., Associate Professor of Education and Program Coordinator of Early Childhood Education, Penn State Harrisburg, 777 West Harrisburg Pike, W314 Olmsted Building, Middletown, Pennsylvania 17057

Dr. Keat taught preschool for many years. Currently, she teaches undergraduate and graduate courses in early childhood education. Her research focuses on teachers as researchers of their own professional practices and teachers as designers of meaningful learning activity in prekindergarten through Grade 3. She has two grown children and five grandchildren.

Mary Napoli, Ph.D., Assistant Professor of Reading and Children's Literature, Penn State Harrisburg, 777 West Harrisburg Pike, W314 Olmsted Building, Middletown, Pennsylvania 17057

Dr. Napoli is a former kindergarten and first-grade classroom teacher. She now teaches undergraduate and graduate courses in children's and young adult literature. Some of her research interests include integrating children's literature across the curriculum and exploring gender and culture in children's literature.

—

Preface

Jane W.:   My children say I live in a different world—a mathematics world!

Jane K.:   My family says I live in a different world—a young child world!

Mary N.:   My friends say I live in a different world—a children's book world!

We have brought our three worlds together in response to the requests of teachers of young children. As we have listened to our teacher friends talk about their mathematics experiences, as children and as educators, we recognize ourselves. Many teachers resemble Jane W., who enjoys thinking about numbers and patterns; she plays with mathematical possibilities simply for the joy of engaging in the process. Many teachers tell us they resemble Jane K., who enjoys thinking with young children; she plays with the child perspectives simply for the joy of engaging in the process. Many teachers tell us they resemble Mary N., who enjoys thinking with storybook characters and contexts; she plays with literature responses simply for the joy of engaging in the process.

The three of us bring similar but different mathematical lenses to our work with teachers and children. Jane K. wishes she had learned about meaningful mathematics when she was a child. Many decades ago, she learned mathematics was memorizing procedures to get the one right answer. Now, Jane K. knows that young children construct knowledge about mathematics all through their early lives.

Jane W. wishes everyone could see and understand that mathematics is around us all of the time. Many decades ago, she learned mathematics was a way of contributing to the world as a means to solve problems, reason logically, and prove numeric and geometric relationships. Now, Jane W. knows young children with mathematical knowledge and problem-solving skills will learn to reason and apply critical thinking all through school and contribute solutions to world problems as adults.

Mary N. wishes all children could enjoy the authentic mathematics that surround characters in storybooks. As a first-grade teacher, she learned that connecting content knowledge to storybooks enhanced children's interest and comprehension. Now, Mary N. knows storybook characters can provide children with access to mathematical knowledge that will extend out into the 22nd century.

What Is the Role of Storybooks in Mathematics?

Storybooks bring children into imaginative worlds where fascinating things happen. They appeal to children's emotions and capture their interest through vivid illustrations, stimulating plots, and exciting characters. By linking mathematics within storybooks, teachers are able to contextualize mathematics by associating it with circumstances and things that occur in the storybook worlds and in children's real worlds. Placing mathematics in a meaningful context helps children relate to mathematics and make sense of the mathematics. Thus, the mathematics becomes real to them, even though it is presented in story. Storybooks speak to children in a way that sparks their curiosity and stimulates their intellect.

What Is Authentic, Meaningful Mathematics for Young Children?

Mathematics is the "search for sense and meaning, patterns and relationships, order and predictability" (Copley, 2000, p. v.). Mathematics is not repetitively enacting a procedure to get a right answer to an irrelevant question. It involves actively engaging young learners in constructing new ideas and helping them reflect on what they are doing and why. Meaningful mathematics entails having young children use manipulatives and number charts to see how numbers and facts are related and help them discover patterns and rules. Mathematics should focus on having children talk about their thinking and have them experience opportunities where they apply reasoning and logic to solve problems. Meaningful mathematical activities mean children make sense of problems and apply various strategies to solve the problems. The problems can be real or imaginary and deal with situations that are meaningful to children. When children can relate to a problem or a character in a story faced with a problem, they are able to think mathematically and see the usefulness of the mathematics.

When Do Children Begin to Think Mathematically?

Infants engage in the process of making sense of the world around them. In order to make sense and meaning, infants must deal with number, shape, size, and patterns. Toddlers know more from less, count, play with toys that provide them practice in evaluating sizes and shapes, and sort items based on classifications such as edible and non-edible (although everything most likely does end up in the mouth!). Preschoolers use mathematical thinking to work imagined and real-world problems by sharing, dividing equally, and figuring out pegboard patterns. Similarly, pre-kindergarten (pre-K) through Grade 3 children solve real life problems as well as assigned mathematics problems. Even more important, young children explore, examine, discover, alter, accommodate, adapt, and question constantly. As they do so, they are searching for meaning, patterns, and interrelationships. In other words, they are engaging in mathematical thinking.

What Can Teachers Do to Enhance Children's Mathematical Thinking?

Children are very inquisitive and want to know about their world. One way teachers can stimulate children's mathematical thinking is by posing open-ended questions that require children to explain or describe a process rather than just give an answer. Limiting the number of lower level questions posed in the classroom and focusing more on higher level questions helps to stimulate their higher order thinking skills. Promoting classroom discourse by having children dialogue with the teacher and with fellow students is also a valuable way to engage children in thinking about their knowledge and understanding. When children are presented with problems that are cognitively demanding, they need to think about the mathematics they know and how it can help them solve the problems. Thus, it is important for all teachers to give children many opportunities to become mentally engaged with the mathematics to develop children's mathematical thinking skills.

The Aim of the Book

This book is written for prospective as well as experienced pre-K–3 teachers who are interested in stimulating children's mathematical thinking by teaching mathematics in a way that encourages children to think about mathematical relationships and solve problems beyond those that emphasize routine procedures. We show how teachers can use storybooks as the context for mathematical problems and questions that are rich and meaningful to children and engage them enthusiastically in mathematical thinking. We also describe the value of teaching mathematics through storybooks and provide examples of how storybooks with playful and imaginative language can promote children's problem-solving skills. Although there are many other subject areas that can be integrated, this book focuses on early literacy, language, and mathematics because many early childhood educators are struggling to meet the demands of these subjects. Our aim is to help prospective and experienced teachers understand

- The need to connect mathematics and emphasize mathematical thinking both within and outside of the allotted time in the day for mathematics

- The ease with which they can connect any storybook to the mathematics curriculum

- The joy and excitement students experience when they are engaged in mathematical problem solving through the context of storybooks

The strategies and examples we provide throughout the book have been implemented in pre-K–3 classrooms and have resulted in positive experiences for both the teachers and students. We hope this book will benefit other pre-K–3 teachers and help them gain confidence with posing mathematical problems and looking for mathematical connections when reading storybooks.

Structure of the Book

The book is divided into two sections: 1) Mathematics and Storybooks and 2) Instructing with Storybooks. Chapter 1 describes mathematics and where we find mathematics. The highlight of the chapter is the true story of one early childhood educator's "aha" moment when she realized that mathematics is all around her and her world. She talks about putting on a new pair of lenses, mathematical lenses, to see patterns, shapes, numeric relationships, and even spatial objects in her everyday life. Chapter 2 focuses on the importance of teaching mathematics beyond skills, computation, and procedures and emphasizes mathematical thinking, reasoning, and problem solving. The chapter addresses key mathematical concepts identified in the National Council of Teachers of Mathematics *Curriculum Focal Points for Prekindergarten through Grade 8 Mathematics: A Quest for Coherence* (2006) and describes how these concepts can be emphasized in storybooks. Chapter 3 describes the role of storybooks and their ability to connect mathematics to children's lives and to their fantasy worlds. It also describes how to select quality storybooks and where to find such books. Chapter 4 discusses how teachers at our workshops struggled to find the mathematics in storybooks and how motivated they were to construct mathematical problems once they were introduced to some approaches we will share in the book.

Section II describes three approaches to using storybooks to pose mathematical problems. Chapter 5 describes the need to emphasize higher level thinking questions and how to pose higher level questions by providing the criteria for higher level questions and showing teachers how to construct higher level questions using Bloom's Taxonomy as a guide. Chapter 6 describes the storybook element approach where teachers use the plot, characters, objects, time frame, setting, and theme of a storybook to set the context for mathematical problems. The chapter includes sample lessons for pre-K–3 in which teachers construct mathematical problems around a storybook.

Chapter 7 describes the curriculum standards approach where teachers identify the curriculum standards they want to address with problems they construct through storybooks. There are two lessons provided for each grade, pre-K–3, with sample teacher scripts. Sample questions and classroom discourse are provided to demonstrate the mathematical ideas explored.

Finally, Chapter 8 describes how mathematical thinking, reasoning, and problem solving can be emphasized in books other than storybooks. This chapter gives information about the use of informational texts and how they can be used to pose mathematical problems. The chapter includes some sample lessons and questions teachers constructed.

We have enjoyed putting together a book that provides opportunities for teachers to make mathematics engaging and meaningful for young children. We hope this book helps you see the value and joy in combining the world of storybooks with the essence of mathematical thinking and understanding.

References

Copely, J.V. (2000). *The young child and mathematics*. Washington, DC: National Association for the Education of Young Children.

National Council of Teachers of Mathematics. (2006). *Curriculum focal points for prekindergarten through Grade 8 mathematics: A quest for coherence*. Reston, VA: Author.

Acknowledgments

This book would not have been possible without the many ideas and input from classroom teachers with whom we have worked. The teachers' enthusiasm for learning how to incorporate storybooks into mathematics and their motivation and willingness to use storybooks in their mathematics classes showed us how important it was for us to share the ideas with a wider audience of classroom teachers. We are also extremely grateful for our family and friends who have supported us along the way and have given us the confidence to complete this book.

Mathematics and Storybooks

 he use of storybooks to pose questions and create scenarios with which to engage students in mathematical thinking may be a novel concept for some teachers of prekindergarten (pre-K) through Grade 3. Many teachers use storybooks to focus classroom discussion on the concept of plot, description of characters, the setting, or possibly the vocabulary. In some cases, teachers use concept books to connect mathematics with literacy by selecting ones that have obvious mathematics throughout, such as counting, shapes, or patterns. But in what ways could teachers select any storybook and pose questions to help students explore mathematical connections or engage them in higher level thinking? What kind of problem-posing scenarios could teachers create from a story to engage students in mathematical questioning or reasoning? How can teachers use storybooks to help cultivate children's mathematical thinking and interest? How can teachers invite storybook characters to accompany children along a path to discover the wonders of the mathematical world? How can teachers polish their own mathematical lens and challenge their students' mathematical thinking so that they can solve problems encountered by characters within a storybook context?

We begin with a story about one teacher who attended the first workshop we presented at a local conference. The first person to enter the room stated emphatically, "*Well, I warn you. I do not like math. I cannot do math. I was always terrible at math.*"

Teachers come to our workshops knowing that mathematics is important. Yet many pre-K–3 teachers say they struggle to find the time to teach mathematics as a result of literacy expectations and increased pressures to meet a growing list of high-stakes standards. Others vividly describe their lack of comfort with teaching mathematics and report that they typically follow the teacher's guide, which often has students completing activities in a workbook or on a worksheet. They describe how students are often disinterested in just doing worksheets. We hear teachers complain that there is often little integration of mathematics with other subjects and little evidence of students engaging in reasoning and problem solving. Often teachers state that they really have no interest in mathematics and tend to not teach in a manner in which they are personally involved in the subject. We hear teachers say that they teach mathematics the same way they were taught, focusing on computation and facts. One teacher explained how she had never been taught to see that mathematics is around us all the time, and she asked, "*If I don't see the math in my world, then how can I help students see the math in their worlds?*"

Mathematics is more than just memorizing facts and following rules or procedures to perform operations such as addition and subtraction. Mathematics is patterns, shapes, equivalence, numbers, relationships, and much more. Mathematics provides recognition, a logic, a vocabulary, a way of reasoning, and opportunities to take an open-minded look at what is and what could be. For centuries, mathematics has been used by people to address and solve real and imagined problems. Who knows how the children of today will use mathematics in their personal and professional lives in the future?

Thus it is important for early childhood teachers to see that mathematics exists in the world around us and is not limited to the pages in a textbook. More important, teachers need to provide opportunities for children to make connections between the mathematics in school and the mathematics in their own world. One way this can be done is by creating problems outside of textbooks, problems that require students to think and make sense of the mathematics needed to solve the problems. By creating problems that children can relate to and that require them to think and make sense of the mathematics needed to solve the problems children become interested in figuring out what to do to solve each problem. As they engage in repeated problem-solving sessions, children apply the mathematics as they learn it. The use of storybooks can set the stage for creating such problems.

The joint position of the National Association for the Education of Young Children (NAEYC) and the National Council of Teachers of Mathematics (NCTM) calls for teachers to find ways to provide the kind of instructional activities in which children continually engage in and construct mathematical knowledge (NAEYC & NCTM, 2002). The call also emphasizes the need to engage children in mathematical explorations in which they use reasoning and problem-solving skills. With this in mind, the goal of this section is to examine the role of mathematics in the early childhood curriculum and the importance of emphasizing reasoning, problem solving, and critical thinking throughout these early grades. We also describe the role of storybooks and examine ways teachers can select quality literature to engage students in mathematical questioning. By integrating storybooks with mathematics, early childhood teachers can plan a comprehensive approach to teaching mathematics, with lessons aligned to state and national standards to enhance student's mathematical abilities in ways that are developmentally, culturally, and individually appropriate. This section invites teachers to put on their mathematical lenses to find mathematics in storybooks and look for opportunities to engage students in meaningful mathematical thinking to solve problems.

CHAPTER 1

What Is Mathematics and Where Is It Found?

eachers of young children are encouraged to design mathematics instruction in ways that are engaging and meaningful. Instruction is *engaging* when children are actively involved in constructing new knowledge by doing, thinking, and talking. Instruction is *meaningful* when children are enthusiastically constructing new knowledge by making connections to their real worlds or to their imaginary worlds. In our workshops with teachers of preschool and primary classes, they have expressed concern that they have rarely experienced engaging and meaningful instruction of mathematics. Furthermore, many teachers have told us that they do not know what mathematics really is, because their mathematics education was so different from what they are now being asked to teach. We recall one teacher who pleaded with us to understand her frustration upon hearing that children need to understand that mathematics is everywhere in the world. We often hear that the teachers have enrolled in our workshop sessions because they know that mathematics is critically important to their children's future and so we work together to answer their questions: What is mathematics? Where is it? We begin with a true story.

Discovering Math in an Airport

Once upon a real time, Jane K. and Jane W. spent several hours in a crowded airport together as a result of icy weather conditions. At first, they passed the time in conversation about personal and professional matters; however, as hour after hour went by, they fell into silence. Eventually, Jane W. said, "*Did you notice that interesting pattern of tiles on the ceiling?*" As Jane K. looked up at the ceiling for the first time, she replied, "*What did you say?*" Jane W. expanded on her question and explained how the design of the ceiling tiles was unusual for this particular shaped room and how fascinated she was with the pattern that had been created there. After an explosion of laughter, Jane K. choked out,

No! I never even noticed the ceiling. I certainly never noticed a pattern there. You are such a math person! Now that I look up, I see the combination of squares and rectangles, but the designers certainly wasted all that effort on me. I wonder what else you have been thinking about as we have been waiting.

Jane W. pointed out the floor tile patterns, described proportional window sizes, reported the various seat arrangement sets, and more. Then Jane W. asked, "*Do you mean to say that you did not notice any of this?*" With more laughter, Jane K. explained,

No! I never saw any of that. Do you want to know what I have been looking at? See those two families over there? I have been noticing how involved those daddies are with their babies. See the dynamics between them as the father smiles and the baby responds? And over there are two women who are engaging their preschoolers in games while they wait. I have been finding all sorts of positive parenting in this crowded place.

This time they both laughed as Jane W. exclaimed, "*You are such an early childhood person!*" They were both stunned by the degree to which they were having such completely different experiences in the same space at the same time. They knew they had experienced an important truth.

This airport experience has become an important moment in our work together. When we came back to campus, we told Mary N. the story. All three of us laughed, of course, and then entered into a serious discussion about the degree to which each of us sees the world through a different lens. Despite the fact that all three of us have spent years reading about and teaching the concept that individuals approach the world from unique perspectives, we were all more keenly aware of the degree to which the two Janes had experienced the same space in the same time frame so differently. Quietly, Jane K. wondered if there might be a connection between her airport experience and her lifelong hazy understanding of mathematics. She noticed that Jane W.'s awareness of mathematics in the airport had absolutely nothing to do with math-as-one-right-answer-to-a-textbook-question that she recalled doing in school many years ago.

Discovering Math Again

Recently, Jane K. and Jane W. were working together by telephone from their homes. As Jane K. discussed a research problem, she glanced out the window. For some reason, she thought, "*Hmm, if Jane W. were looking out this window, she would probably see math in that oak tree or in the hedge or in the telephone pole.*" As Jane K. continued to look out the window, her perception changed and she suddenly saw the window differently. Abruptly, she saw that the window was actually made up of two windows, each of which comprised 8 small panes of glass that made up a total of 16 panes of glass. In a flash, she actually saw the patterns of glass within the two larger rectangles, and then she became aware of the two rectangular curtain panels on either side of the window. There was a pattern in the window frame that she never noticed. In another flash, she became aware that these window rectangles actually were in the middle of a wall that was also in the shape of a rectangle. To her surprise, she noted that the window screens were rectangles too, and in a tumble of thought, she saw rectangles everywhere in the room. In this very room that had been her office for 21 years, in the house that had been her home for 40 years, Jane K. saw mathematics everywhere. The blinds formed rectangles. The bookcases were rectangles. Most of the books were rectangles. The ceiling and all the walls were rectangles, as well as the doors, the window seat cushion, the desk surface, the file cabinets, and the rug.

In another tumble of awareness, she saw angles. She laughed as she thought, *"I have never seen an angle anywhere in my life, and now there are angles all over this office."* The experience was almost dizzying—in terms of seeing what she had not seen before. At this point, she described her altered perception to Jane W. She added,

I am reminded of those movie houses where they give you special glasses that alter what you see. Have you tried on those glasses that change the perception of a two-dimensional screen so that you see in a three-dimensional manner? Well, I feel as though I have put on math lenses, and I see geometry all over this room!

Jane W. was fascinated to hear that Jane K. could finally see the mathematics that had been there all along—the mathematics that Jane W. would have seen immediately. Silently, Jane K. became more certain that there was a connection between her lack of mathematics awareness and her lifelong hazy understanding of mathematics.

Where Is Mathematics in Teachers' Lives?

When we told Mary N. about this experience, we remembered together the comments of many preschool and primary school teachers we have met in our workshops and classes. Many teachers see the world in Jane K.'s way, without a math lens. Yet 21st-century teachers recognize that they are responsible for helping children see the world the way Jane W. does, with mathematical lenses that illuminate mathematical awareness in every aspect of a child's life.

Furthermore, teachers have expressed discomfort in knowing that despite the critical importance of mathematics to their children's future, it is the content area about which they feel the least confident. They know they must develop children's ability to engage in mathematical reasoning and problem solving, but they continue to teach in much the same way as they were taught—with calendars and worksheets. Therefore, it is apparent to us that children continue to see mathematics as something one does during mathematics time—usually to get a right answer by completing a set of steps that focus on skills and procedures.

In contrast, many other teachers have well-developed mathematical lenses. They tell us that they know that mathematics is much bigger than chapters in books or activities to be completed. They know that mathematics is problem solving, inquiry, and thinking logically. It is relationships between numbers, patterns, and shapes and having number sense to decompose and compose numbers. Essentially, mathematical understanding is necessary to be able to solve world, business, academic, and everyday problems. It is our view that children benefit from learning with teachers who put on a mathematical lens and begin to see the mathematics in their worlds and can pose problems that promote inquiry.

Stop and Look for the Mathematics

Readers, we invite you to intentionally open your eyes to the mathematics that is in your space right now. In other words, we ask you to construct or focus your mathematical lens. We ask you to stop reading and take a moment to look around the room and find various shapes, patterns of shapes, various sizes of objects, relationships of various-sized objects, quantities of objects, and patterns of quantities. Readers, to enhance your ability to create meaningful mathematics problems for students, we suggest that, while wearing a mathematics lens, you take a moment to be aware of a few meaningful adult mathematical problems you have addressed related to the space you are in now. Perhaps you see the mathematics involved in choosing the right table for your porch. Perhaps you have figured out how many cans of paint are needed to paint the walls in a room. As adults enhance awareness of the potential for mathematical reasoning in their everyday lives, they are likely to increase their ability to construct problems for children in which they need to apply problem-solving skills and mathematical thinking.

Stop and Look a Moment into Children's Lives

Readers, we now invite you to intentionally open your eyes to the mathematics that is in your children's worlds. In other words, we ask you to construct or focus your mathematical lens slightly differently. Like Jane K., if you think about mathematics with a geometry lens, then you may find that there are rectangles and angles and circles and spheres all over the classroom where you have been teaching for many years. As an early childhood educator, you might also think about the mathematics potential that surrounds each child and family. Suddenly, you might recognize the mathematics potential of the adults in children's families, their siblings, their extended family members, neighbors, and pets.

Like Jane W., you might think about mathematics with multiple mathematical lenses. For example, you might think about your school building with a measurement lens and discover new reasons to measure new spaces (e.g., halls, doors, windows, desks, tiles, panes, radiators). Of course, you might look for the mathematics in your school neighborhood with an algebra lens and discover problems related to patterns of lamp posts, sidewalk squares, front porches, bushes, trees, clouds, and more. If you wonder with your students, you all might decide to show the children in the class across the hall what you discovered, and then you will need to represent your mathematical discoveries in some way. The children are likely to have unique ideas about why and how to organize and draw your discoveries so that others can see your thoughts regarding what was found. Of course, you might quickly begin to think about the mathematical potential of inviting children to think about quantity issues, spatial concerns, size comparisons, and recurring patterns in children's lives.

Like Mary N., you might quickly leave the mathematics in a child's actual world and begin to think about the mathematics in a child's imaginary world through storybooks that children love to hear or read. You may find yourself thinking about the number of train engines that would not help *The Little Engine that Could* (Piper, 1976). By incorporating a Jane W. mathematical sense, you might also think about time problems, space concerns, measurement necessities, and relative size concerns. I have often wondered how the smallest engine could pull such a heavy load, but one of the larger train engines said it could not do so. Alternately, you might think about the spatial issues in *A Chair for My Mother* (Williams, 1982) or measurement issues surrounding the sons of the tailor father in *A Cloak for the Dreamer* (Friedman, 1994). You might recognize mathematical potential that you had not seen before during the multiple times that you and your students have enjoyed the stories, characters, contexts, plots, and themes of a familiar book. Over the past 5 years, teachers we have worked with have reported an abrupt sense of surprise when they see for the first time the mathematical potential that had been there all along in their classroom and read-alouds. When teachers in our workshop sessions metaphorically put on or focus their mathematical lenses, they often erupt in laughter and relief as a result of perceiving the logical and natural connections between storybooks and mathematical curriculum concepts.

The next chapter is designed to polish teachers' mathematical lenses by finding, defining, and playing with mathematical concepts and processes that surround children's lives, homes, and classrooms during their preschool and primary years.

CHAPTER 2

Mathematics in a Child's World

child's world is filled with the big ideas of mathematics such as numbers, shapes, pictures, and symbols. "Mathematics is essentially the search for sense and meaning, patterns and relationships, order and predictability" (Copley, 2000, p. v.). With this definition of mathematics as a sense-making activity, one can see that young children are natural mathematicians. Infants search faces and voices for familiar patterns, and toddlers recognize and rely on predictable routines and time sequences. Preschoolers categorize and classify familiar items according to various criteria, and kindergartners understand the phonics meanings of letters and the quantity meaning of numerals. Finally, children in Grades 1, 2, and 3 continue to develop sense-making skills of more and more abstract symbols.

Discovering Mathematics in a Workshop

We begin our discussion of mathematics in the world of a child with a story about one teacher who attended the first workshop we presented. While we were nervously preparing the room for our workshop session, the first two teachers entered the room. They were laughing and seemed even more nervous than we were. The taller teacher announced,

Well, I have to tell you, I hate math! I have never been good at math! In fact, I have always been terrible at math! So good luck with me. I doubt there is anything you can do with me, but here I am!

At this point, the shorter teacher explained,

We are both so bad at math. All through school, we just could not get it. My grades were so bad; I don't tell anyone about them. I would be embarrassed if the parents of the children I teach now knew about my grades then. So we are

here because we have state math standards that we have to help our students meet. I hate to say it, but I feel fearful about teaching math because I do not want to mess up my kids by teaching them wrong. But I know I am not teaching them enough.

At this point, other teachers began to enter the workshop session. The taller teacher moved to the back row of chairs, saying, *"Like I said, good luck with me. I doubt you can help us with math, but we can always say we tried."*

We were relieved that several teachers entered the room telling us that they had always been good at mathematics and loved to teach their students in new and innovative ways. We began our workshop session with the knowledge that participants brought a range of mathematical knowledge and skill levels. In other words, some participants viewed mathematics through lenses like those of Jane K., whereas others were able to view mathematics through lenses like Jane W.'s.

As we read from storybooks and demonstrated the mathematics slightly hidden within the story and illustrations, session participants began to build upon our ideas with suggestions of their own. Each pair of teachers shared storybooks that we had brought to the workshop to examine for evidence of mathematics. We were pleased when we heard a teacher exuberantly say, *"I found geometry in here!"* Another teacher said just as loudly, *"Well, there are numbers in all the books, right? But I found a pattern—so that's algebra—right?"*

When we heard the first teacher to enter the room shout, *"I can do this!"* in a voice so loud no one could miss it, tears sprang to our eyes. We moved to the back row so she could show us what she meant, and through her own tears, she said,

I can do this! I can ask children about anything in a book—including numbers, shapes, sizes, spaces, time, money, and quantities. I do this kind of thing all of the time, not with math, but with all sorts of problems that characters might struggle with. I am always saying, "Well, I wonder what would happen if this character did this or that." And I am always asking the kids to think about how the story might change if something else happened. All I have to do now is look at the math curriculum and have the character do math things or face math struggles.

Again and again, she exclaimed, *"I can do this!"*

The enthusiasm of this teacher changed us. After the session, we went to Jane K.'s house to talk about what had happened. We noted that this teacher seemed to have found a form of mathematics that made sense to her and that she could confidently relate to her students. As she was leaving, she confided to Jane W. that she had never known that mathematics fit into actual life, much less imaginary life. She said she thought mathematics was a step to an answer that no one needed to know. Moreover, she explained that she had always had a strong sense that mathematics was more than that, but the way she was asked to teach mathematics *"felt the same as the way I had learned math—just do and say what you are supposed to do and say."* In contrast, she told Jane W., *"Now I see that math is actually thinking; I have probably been thinking with math all my life and not knowing it."*

In this first workshop teachers asked us when children can begin to think mathematically. With child care teachers in the workshop session, we all thought together about infants, toddlers, preschoolers, kindergartners, and children in the primary Grades 1, 2, and 3. Very early in life, children's natural curiosity drives their exploration of everything. Using all five senses, young children taste, smell, listen, look, and touch objects in order to comprehend their surroundings. By exploring shapes, thickness, softness, musical toys, stackable objects, and so forth, they learn to characterize objects according to various attributes. Initial sorting experiences such as putting away toys and groceries help them learn about sets and how to categorize and sort. These self-directed activities provide young children with the foundational knowledge needed for mathematics.

In addition to sensory explorations, older toddlers and preschoolers extend sense making by engaging in imaginary play. Through their imaginations, children try out possibilities and correct inaccuracies about concepts of quantity, shape, spatial awareness, size, patterns, data analysis, and representation. Children in kindergarten and the primary grades continue to explore mathematical concepts and skills by examining real-life and imaginary items, images, and symbols in their games, friendships, and sibling interactions. The unique nature of each child's exploration opportunities and developmental schedule ensures that children enter school with differing conceptual acquisitions and gaps.

Adult Role in Child Mathematical Thinking

Before children enter school, many will have engaged in meaningful interactions with adults who have intentionally facilitated the development of concepts of quantity, time, coins, shapes, measurement, and sequence. Piaget identified this early type of knowledge as *logico-mathematical*, meaning that children's brains create relationships on the basis of other previously understood relationships. This internal knowledge develops from experiences as children match, order, count, and compare. Children cannot see *two*, but they develop the understanding of "twoness" from relationships they form as we have them count, talk, and think about the mental construct of *two*. Adults who foster children's mathematical development often engage in experiences in which there is conversation as well as exploration about patterns in floor tiles, shapes of floor tiles, numbers on a clock, the number of petals on a flower, and so forth. Children's learning is further enhanced when adults guide their thinking by posing questions to scaffold child discovering, wondering, and comprehending (Vygotsky, 1978). As adults talk about underlying mathematical relationships, children extend their knowledge base and expand their comprehension level.

Parents play an important role in helping children think about mathematical concepts and relationships. Many parents intentionally scaffold when they encourage their children to count items around the house, estimate number of steps, compare sizes of items in a cupboard, build structures with blocks, and look for patterns around a room. Moreover, parents can pose questions that require children to think and to use their developing language to express what they are thinking. Highlighting patterns that occur in nursery rhymes, storybooks, songs, routines, and objects can help children learn foundational skills for algebraic reasoning. Family members who help children develop a mathematical lens with which to see various relationships and become aware of the mathematics surrounding them will enable the children to connect to the mathematical concepts they will learn during their school years.

Early childhood teachers are in a position to continue to help children make these mathematical connections and develop mathematical relationships. Activities such as pointing out mathematics in the classroom or school, creating mathematical problems, and playing games that involve some number concepts or the use of logic and strategy encourage children to see that mathematics is everywhere. For example, when teachers talk with their pre-K students about the number of children present and the number of children absent, each child is invited to think mathematically about the real world of the classroom. In addition, when teachers ask second graders to predict how much snow fell on the playground the previous day, discuss how to measure the actual snowfall, and consider how to compare the difference between prediction and actual snow accumulation, each child is thinking mathematically about the real world in the classroom. If students begin to see the world through mathematical eyes, they will be able to engage in mathematical explorations and use mathematical reasoning all day long. As teachers, it is important to promote the fact that we use mathematical reasoning in various ways, and we use numbers and counting in daily routines.

We want children to be exposed to rich experiences in which they need to explain how they found an answer or make conjectures regarding how they arrived at an answer to a question. Mathematics in a child's world may involve using concepts such as numbers, operations, patterns, shapes, measurement, data, estimation, graphing, equivalence, and position. Teachers need to guide children's learning of mathematics and expose them to different mathematical concepts in various situations throughout the day. It is especially important for teachers to pose questions that encourage children to use different strategies to solve problems and then talk about the ways in which they solved the problem. By posing questions such as these, teachers can help students develop their mathematical understanding and mathematical language.

Problem Solving

Children's cognitive abilities are more sophisticated than research by Piaget first suggested (Sophian, 1999). Children are capable of engaging in advanced content typically not addressed in preschool curricula (Ginsburg, Inoue, & Seo, 1999). They are able to apply various problem-solving strategies, although somewhat inconsistently, and engage in higher level thinking. Thus mathematical learning in the early grades must also emphasize problem-solving experiences and higher level thinking. Typically, problems that require children to compare and contrast, generalize, and predict involve more cognitive ability than those that require children to perform operations such as addition or subtraction.

Most textbooks pose word or "story" problems that require students to write number sentences and find the answer. These problems put mathematics in a context and help students learn to read and interpret mathematical statements and apply mathematical operations. Although these types of problems play an important role in the curriculum, they do not promote the true meaning of mathematical problem solving as defined by *An Agenda for Action* (Edwards, 1980). In this document, Edwards called for mathematics instructional programs to teach mathematics through problem solving in which students need to think, analyze, and apply known or invented strategies. The problems should arise in a context and require students to make connections to previously learned mathematical concepts.

For example, in a first-grade classroom, a teacher who has already taught concepts regarding measurement might alert her students to the fact that the class across the hall wants to find out if both classrooms have the same-size desks, tables, and chairs. How would one find out the answer to this question? Let's pretend that the class across the hall wants to make this a more difficult problem, so they say that measuring with rulers is not allowed. How might the answer to their question be determined with using rulers? This could lead to a discussion of same and different units of measure as well as several experiments involving what happens when the same and different units of measure are used. Teachers who see mathematics the way Jane K. does, with no mathematical lens, have told us that they have learned along with their students to search their classrooms for interesting questions regarding number, operations, shapes, spatial awareness, measurement, patterns, and data representation.

When problems are posed in a context that is meaningful and appears real to students, they are more motivated to solve them. In the pre-K–3 curriculum, the best problems are those that capture students' interest and relate to their world, either real or imaginary. Problems that are open-ended and can be solved in more than one way lend themselves to more mathematical thinking than problems that are closed and have a set answer.

It is important to embed these types of problems into the curriculum daily and not necessarily just in the mathematics curriculum. These problems can be posed while discussing science, health, music, and social studies. Throughout this book, we show how open-ended problems can be embedded in the reading curriculum through storybooks. The more opportunities teachers can find to engage students in mathematical problem solving throughout the day, the more students will begin to see this as a way of thinking rather than just something you do during mathematics class.

Posing Problems

It is important for teachers to gain confidence and begin to see that they have the ability to create and pose mathematical problems. Although textbooks are a great resource for word problems, people need to put on mathematical lenses and see the mathematics that surrounds them in their everyday lives as a resource for problems. Some pre-K–3 teachers may not feel as if they are competent in mathematics beyond the grade level they are teaching; however, they can learn to pose interesting and stimulating mathematics problems and think mathematically about a situation. With some practice, this ability to construct and pose an open-ended problem related to lifelike situations can become second nature. In our initial work with teachers, we found that many were able to construct typical word or story problems that required specific basic operations to solve, and yet the idea of constructing an open-ended problem was at first not as easy. However, many teachers found that once they started constructing some open-ended problems, they felt as if they were on a roll and were surprised at how easily and quickly they could create many mathematical problems related to context and people who were meaningful to the children. They gained confidence in their ability to pose a problem that they had not even thought about before and for which they had no idea what the answer was before asking students to solve it. They found they could easily start a problem by saying, "I wonder . . . " or "What if . . . " even if they did not know the answer.

Our work with pre-K–3 teachers helped us realize how motivated the teachers became in constructing open-ended problems once they began to understand that mathematical problem solving was not solving word problems. In one case, a teacher asked her students how they could find out how many students were in the school. She realized she was more interested in the ideas they had about how to find the answer rather than the answer itself. This teacher has invited the children in her class to think mathematically about their real world of school. The teachers started to see how having students engage in the guess-and-check strategy was mathematically powerful when they asked students to think about what could be a "good" guess and why.

Curriculum Focal Points

Pre-K–3 mathematics instruction needs to be more than teaching skills and procedures. Rather, it should focus on helping develop children's conceptual understanding of key concepts and teaching them how to generalize and transfer knowledge to other mathematical situations. In 2006, NCTM released *Curriculum Focal Points for Prekindergarten Through Grade 8 Mathematics: A Quest for Coherence* (2006). In the focal points, NCTM identified essential mathematics designed to represent instructional goals and desirable learning expectations rather than specific objectives. Three focal points were highlighted for each grade level, along with the need for emphasis on problem solving, reasoning, and critical thinking skills. For example, the kindergarten focal points highlight the mathematical topics of representing, comparing, and ordering whole numbers and joining and separating sets; describing shapes and space; and ordering objects by measurable attributes. The goal is that by organizing a curriculum around the focal points, students will gain deep understanding of mathematical concepts and relationships.

We had pre-K–3 teachers look at the focal points and the desired learning expectations for their grade level. To facilitate the goal of helping teachers promote more mathematical problem solving, we asked teachers to focus on one focal point and read the description of the key concepts. Then we asked them to select a storybook—any storybook—and read it with the intent of finding a character or a situation in the story around which they could pose a mathematical problem. We describe this process in more detail in Chapter 6, but what is important to recognize here is the success teachers began having in constructing problems from a storybook when they had to frame a problem around a particular mathematical concept.

Identifying this focal point and then finding an opportunity or situation in the story where the mathematics could be found enabled teachers to see how to connect mathematics to the storybook. It was easier to construct a problem when the mathematics that was to be embedded was obvious to them. Also, the teachers found that they could construct different problems that allowed students to use various strategies or in some cases invent strategies to solve a problem. Problems such as these require students to think about the mathematics and not just perform a routine algorithm or operation. Making sense of the problem is the first step—and an important step—to being able to solve the problem. When the problem is posed from the context of a storybook or from the story's characters, teachers find that the students want to understand it better than when they read a problem in a text (Seifert, 1993). In our studies, teachers reported that children's interest and enthusiasm for mathematics significantly increased after teaching a unit on money through storybooks (Wilburne et al., 2007).

Problems in Context

Posing problems within a meaningful context to children through storybooks is one way to make mathematics real and engaging. By relying on the innate capacity of young children to pretend, teachers found that they could have students think about a mathematical problem they might face inside the storybook world or a problem one of the storybook characters might encounter. The teachers were able to take story characters out of the books and into the children's bedrooms, kitchens, or community to create mathematical problems. This way of thinking helped the teachers pose more "what if" questions to launch students' mathematical thinking. For example, a teacher reading the book *Benny's Pennies* (Brisson, 1995) posed problems such as, "*What if Benny wanted to give you 10 cents? How many coins could he give you?*" and "*What if Benny put a penny in his bank every day for a month (or a year)? How much money would he have saved?*"

The everyday lives of children typically consist of different routines and traditions. Some children spend their free time in sporting activities, dance, music lessons, or video games. Their families enjoy different foods and celebrate different holidays. The challenge for teachers is how to contextualize mathematics in terms that are familiar to all students. One benefit to using storybooks as the context for mathematics is that all students can relate to the storybook world or the characters in the story. The stories can connect to children's fantasy worlds and their imaginations. It is in their imaginations that the mathematics becomes meaningful. We found that it was helpful when teachers had an understanding of their children's interests and favorite things to do and read storybooks that addressed these topics. All children, regardless of race, socioeconomic status, or ability, can enjoy the stimulation and fascination of using mathematical thinking to solve a problem for an imaginary character from a storybook.

Cultural Diversity

Storybooks provide opportunities to explore culture and cultural diversity with characters who are in various parts of the world and fantasy world (National Council for the Social Studies, 1997). Teachers can use multicultural literature as a medium for embracing cultural traditions and mathematical thinking. Multicultural literature offers a context in which students can celebrate their personal cultures and learn from others to make meaningful connections between their own

experiences and the story. Banks (1994) indicated that education in a diverse society should affirm and help students understand their home and community cultures and free them from cultural boundaries. Thus, for students from another
country or identified as English as a Second Language (ESL) learners, teachers
can integrate global literature and scaffold students' learning by paying close
attention to pictures, creative drawings, or illustrations to accompany problem-
posing explorations. Moreover, teachers can use real objects, storybooks audio
recorded, storytelling activities, and the language experience approach to provide
ESL/immigrant students with opportunities to develop language skills and explore mathematics. Incorporating high-quality selections of multicultural literature provides students with rich language exposure and helps them value their
cultural histories.

Language and Mathematics

Storybooks provide opportunities for children to learn the language of the story
and connect it to the language of mathematics. This emphasis on language is critical in helping children make sense of mathematics and think about what they are
doing. Having students discuss their problem-solving processes and strategies
with other students and dialogue with adults plays a vital role in their learning of
complex mathematical concepts (Vygotsky, 1978). By communicating their mathematical ideas and expressing their thinking through language, students benefit
in terms of their own learning as well as that of their fellow students.

We found that posing mathematics problems through storybooks increased
children's use of vocabulary and language. By posing a mathematics problem
through a character in a story, the children were excited to explain how they
solved the problem to the character. In a kindergarten classroom, a teacher told
the students that Benny from *Benny's Pennies* (Brisson, 1995) was given 10¢ by
his uncle, who insisted on a detailed report of how Benny spent the money. So
Benny had to figure out how he could spend 10¢ in buying certain items the
teacher had drawn on chart paper. Pencils were 2¢, erasers were 3¢, and crayons
were 4¢. The students explained how Benny could purchase five pencils, two
erasers and a crayon, two crayons and a pencil, and so forth. The teacher also had
them prove their answers to Benny by writing the appropriate number sentences.
As the students discussed how they found their answers, they were addressing
Benny rather than their teacher. One kindergarten teacher shared how she encouraged the students to use mathematical terms so that Benny would know what
they were talking about. For instance, rather than saying "*I just added the two
numbers,*" she encouraged them to explain to Benny what you call the two numbers. As one student readjusted his explanation, he said to Benny and to the class,
"*I added the two addends and found a sum of 10.*" Inviting children to think
about mathematics with the imaginative part of their mind is often more effective
than inviting children to think about mathematics only with the rational, logical
part of their mind (Schiro, 2004). The power of storybooks taps into their imaginary world and provides a stimulus for rich mathematical conversations. Getting
students to talk about mathematics and explain their thinking is essential to their
learning and understanding.

The Primary Mathematics Curriculum

Primary curricula programs differ in their approach to teaching mathematics. Some materials provide explicit instruction for teachers to follow, whereas others give a mix of teacher- and child-guided activities. Programs also differ in how concepts are presented. Some programs introduce concepts linearly and in progressively increasing depth; others have spiral curricula, which means that concepts are discussed several times throughout the program, with varying degrees of depth. Despite the type of curricula program used by the teachers with whom we worked, they wanted assistance in talking with children as naturally about mathematical ideas as about read-aloud ideas.

As we worked with teachers, we found it necessary to develop several frameworks to help teachers think about finding the mathematics in storybooks and connect it to their curriculum. Through the frameworks, teachers were able to use the plot, characters, and setting of the story to be the context for a mathematics problem. They were also able to choose a mathematics concept or focal point and think about how they could have a character in the story be faced with a problem around that concept. The more teachers tried to create mathematics problems, the easier it became for them. They started responding positively to connecting a mathematical activity to a storybook and discussed how they would focus on the children's problem-solving ability. They looked to create open-ended problems that required students to think and use a variety of strategies to solve the problem. As the teachers created problems, they found that the problems were more interesting to the students than some of the problems in their curriculum. These storybook problems promoted rich discussions among the students when they shared their strategies or explained their solutions. The teachers expressed how the dialog was richer and more interactive between students and between the teacher and students when they discussed problems from the storybook. This excited the teachers and helped them realize the importance of going beyond the textbook to engage students in mathematical discovery and problem solving.

CHAPTER 3

The World of Storybooks

he world of storybooks is truly a treasure for children. Once we open the pages of a favorite storybook, we experience the joy of watching our young children's expressions gleam with delight as they embark on new adventures, meet new storybook friends, and explore new ideas. Through a story, children's imaginations soar while nourishing their sense of curiosity and wonder. So, how do we define a storybook, and what have we learned are the qualities of good stories for young children?

A storybook communicates its message through both illustrations and words. Storybooks are rich in literary language and contain gorgeous and varied illustrations to provide young readers with a sense of the elements that comprise good literature. In Cyndi Giorgis' and Joan Glazer's (2009) book, *Literature for Young Children: Supporting Emergent Literacy*, they suggested that one way to analyze fiction is to explore the literary elements that are inherent to the selection. These include:

 PLOT: Good storybooks contain well-developed plots that are interesting, engaging, and logical.

 SETTING: The location of where events take place is an integral part of the story. Writers often include descriptors to help readers identify with the setting. Settings that are authentic, accurate, and interesting are well loved by readers.

CHARACTERIZATION: Ask a young child about characters such as Olivia, Eloise, Max, or Fancy Nancy, and they will be able to share what they know about them. Good characters are memorable for young readers because the writer creates descriptions about them. Well-defined characters, whether human or animal, are presented in a way that enables readers to connect to a character's personality traits and to talk about what they like or dislike about the character.

THEME: The underlying message of the story is understood as its theme. Many times, the theme can be as simple as learning how to be a good friend or sibling. The theme is an integral feature of the story but should not overshadow the story in any way.

STYLE: Authors employ a variety of literary and language devices to whet their readers' appetites for words. A good storybook is rich in language and descriptions that are a natural part of the story. The language that is employed in a well-written storybook is vivid, evokes rich images of the actions, and reflects the mood of the characters and overall story.

A well-written storybook will leave the reader satisfied with the way in which the characters are presented, the inherent dialogue, and the way illustrations add to the overall story. Storybooks cover a wide range of topics and themes often based on everyday experiences that children can easily identify, such as sharing, dealing with emotions, and learning about family. Reading aloud quality storybooks with young readers presents opportunities for them to co-construct meaning and explore values, beliefs, and attitudes. Jalongo (2004) explained in her book, *Young Children and Picture Books*, that storybooks are a major resource for supporting children's social, emotional, and intellectual development. Storybooks can be found in every genre, from traditional literature and realistic fiction to fantasy and historical fiction. The many types of storybooks available enable teachers to meet the varying needs and interests of their students.

Storybooks provide a wonderful introduction to engage students in mathematical explorations and mathematical thinking. Some storybooks have obvious mathematics-related plots or contexts. In these cases, teachers find they can easily pose questions directly from the text or create extensions to the mathematics in the story. One classic example of a storybook with numbers is *The Doorbell Rang* (Hutchins, 1986). This lively book effectively conveys the concepts of sharing and simple mathematics to young children. Before reading the story, students can predict what will happen in the story by pondering questions such as: What are the children (characters) doing? Why are they gathered around the door? During reading, students can count how many times the doorbell rings (problem) and how many children visit Victoria and Sam's house. They can look at the patterns found in the number of doorbell rings and predict how many children would be at the house after 10 rings or 20 rings. After reading, the students can discuss the concept of sharing (theme) and use manipulative cookies (or real ones) to reenact the story before posing their own problems.

In other cases, a storybook may have no obvious or apparent mathematical connections. The storybook may be one that connects to children's lives, has an interesting plot, or teaches a moral. It is just as important to consider using these books to engage children in mathematical thinking and problem solving because of their potential to show how mathematical reasoning and thinking are skills that can be used in all contexts. If we only pose mathematical problems when we read storybooks with numbers or shapes, children may identify these books as mathematics books. We want children to understand that mathematics is not just a subject; rather, it is a mental process that involves thinking about relationships, visualizing and understanding representations, reasoning, and problem solving.

Concept Books and Storybooks

We found many pre-K–3 teachers who stated that they used concept books that emphasized counting, numbers, or specific mathematical topics to connect reading to mathematical concepts. According to Carlson (1996, p. 53), a concept book can be defined as "a book intended for a child that focuses on colors, shapes, sizes, numbers and counting, and the alphabet." Several examples of concept books the teachers used were *12 Ways to Get to 11* (Merriam, 1993), *The Coin Counting Book* (Williams, 2001), and *The Jelly Bean Fun Book* (Capucilli, 2001). The teachers noted that they found minimal opportunities to pose problems with the concept books that were open-ended or required their children to use various strategies to solve.

The teachers had not thought to use storybooks with a plot, characters, and a setting to have their children become intellectually involved in thinking about mathematics, physically involved in doing mathematics, and emotionally involved with the impact that the book's mathematics might have on its characters or on the children's own lives (Schiro, 1997). If the mathematics was not obvious in the story, the teachers failed to see how to integrate the book into a mathematics lesson. As children connect stories to their own lives, they often integrate other content areas, too. After trying to use the storybook, *Swimmy* (Lionni, 1973) to engage children in mathematics, one preschool teacher explained,

I was surprised how long the children talked about the problems encountered, when I thought they would be more involved with the illustrated pictures in a concept book. One boy continued to reread, touch the one little black fish, and ask questions about Swimmy long after I had finished using the book to teach about sets of numbers. For many days, this child asked us to count and recount all the many smaller fish—all the red fish—and then he would solemnly ask, "He is the leader? Look, he is the only black one, and he is the leader." This child was clearly thinking in sets, but he was also thinking about more than sets.

The NCTM promotes the collaboration of reading and mathematics and asserts that reading children's literature and connecting it to mathematics needs more emphasis in the K–4 curriculum (NCTM, 2000). When carefully selected and meaningfully shared, children's storybooks provide a rich context for promoting mathematical connections. The plot and characters in storybooks invite young children to imagine, query, guess, infer, predict, and pose questions. The beauty of the storybook language is infused into the learning, providing a rich context for teaching mathematics and literacy. The visual representations in storybooks provide a natural connection to engage young learners in mathematical thinking and language. The language and narrative context of a storybook invite the young learner to explore problems and wonder about mathematical ideas.

Children are motivated and stimulated to solve mathematical problems when they are presented in the context of a storybook. Their ability to pretend and imagine enables them to become emotionally involved with the storybook and enter into the storybook world. In this world, the mathematics appears relevant as opposed to mathematics taught as expository instruction (Seifert, 1993). The context of the storybook is familiar, relevant, and interesting to children, making the mathematics more meaningful. Research confirms that young children learn more effectively in settings that are familiar to them and when the learning is in a context that is meaningful for them (Althouse, 1994; Copple & Bredekamp, 2009; Good & Brophy, 1987).

Enthusiasm and Engagement

Hyson (2008) summarized recent research on the characteristics and traits that young children exhibit when they learn well. She reported two main categories: enthusiasm and engagement. Furthermore, she identified three elements of the enthusiasm category: interest, pleasure, and motivation to learn. Moreover, she identified four elements of the engagement category: attention, persistence, flexibility, and self-regulation. Teachers consistently report that young children enthusiastically engage in read-aloud time. One of the reasons teachers enjoy read-aloud time in the school day is the degree of interest, pleasure, motivation, attention, persistence, flexibility, and self-regulation the children consistently demonstrate.

We found many teachers of young children who expressed confidence in their ability to integrate story comprehension with writing activities, social studies questions, science inquiries, and more. One kindergarten teacher said,

I think my favorite part of the day is the discussion after a read-aloud, when I am asking questions to check on the children's comprehension. This is when I can really see how they think—like when I read A Chair for My Mother *(Williams, 1982). Some children talked only about the fire; others talked about sharing, saving money, parents' jobs, new household things, extended family members, and more.*

Selecting Quality Storybooks

Storybooks provide opportunities for teachers to make mathematics authentic and meaningful. In selecting storybooks, we suggest choosing ones that exhibit all the qualities of good literature. For example, in *Little Chick* (Hest, 2009), children will be delighted by three stories about Little Chick's relationship with her "Old-Auntie," an encouraging and maternal hen. Little Chick embodies the social and emotional developmental characteristics of imagining and wanting things to happen quickly, such as making her carrot grow and her kite fly. But with the gentle nudge and encouragement of Old-Auntie, Little Chick realizes that while she cannot always immediately do what she wants, there are many things she can do with splendid skill. She realizes that she is a good and patient gardener, she can skip with a nice bounce, and she is a good stretcher. The three stories showcase two charming characters in a warm and loving relationship. The language is simple, yet rich with emotional description. The illustrations by Anita Jeram are soft, muted watercolors highlighting the loving connection of the characters and make the story come alive. For example, the picture of Old-Auntie gently placing her wing over Little Chick and protecting her in a "blanket of love" is very beautiful and holds a significant message for readers. The characterization and the plots in each story capture the importance caregivers have in children's lives. Moreover, the theme of the story explores the fact that sometimes individuals' attempts to achieve the impossible provide them with important lessons about themselves.

In addition to selecting high-quality literature, teachers can discover that mathematical problems and concepts can be explored within the context of the story. As we read storybooks together with young children, we can ask them to predict what will happen, explore a character's problems, and invite them into the world of the story. Hunsader (2004, p. 618) pointed out that "engagement with literature provides a natural way for students to connect the abstract language of mathematics to their personal world." Teachers of young children typically organize their literacy block with interactive read-alouds and shared reading; therefore, as storybooks are integrated across the curriculum, teachers can model purposeful literacy strategies with children while encouraging mathematical thinking.

Teachers have many outlets to find high-quality books from professional organizations, book lists, book fairs, and web sites. There is a list of resources and web sites for selecting high-quality storybooks included at the end of this book. Throughout this book, we help you learn how to select any storybook to stimulate children's mathematical thinking and pose mathematical inquiries.

CHAPTER 4

Becoming Motivated to Find the Mathematics

s soon as I get home from this conference, I am going directly to *my book closet at school. There has been math hiding in my books all these years, and I never found it. No more! It was so much fun finding the math here together, I think I will see if my team would like to do this together. Just look how we all laughed as we found ways to get Corduroy and all these other characters into math trouble so the children can think them out of the problems. If we mark our books with math questions, the whole team will be set when school starts again.*

This exuberant teacher sparked the other participants to make plans about marking bookshelf books with problem-posing questions.

In addition, this teacher prompted Jane W., Jane K., and Mary N. to try her suggestion. Her eagerness to get together with colleagues to share stories, enjoy illustrations, and find potential mathematical problems for the characters led us to an upstairs room in our campus library. With snacks and coffee, a huge pile of recently released storybooks, and a list of mathematics standards for our state (Pennsylvania), we set to work—reading, wondering, imagining, thinking, posing, and laughing. After about an hour, we began to recognize that the quality of our laughter seemed to be connected to the quality of our creativity and the pure enjoyment of freely imagining what could happen to the characters created by authors and illustrators. Jane K. remembered playing with ideas in this way when she taught preschoolers. Mary N. remembered playing with ideas in this way when she taught first grade. Jane W. remembered playing with ideas with adolescents in middle and high school settings. All three recalled the recent words of Thomas Friedman (2005), who pointed out that the most important resource in the United States is the creativity of its people. In the moment that we recognized that creativity and mathematics are important on the national and global scene, the laughter stopped. Suddenly, we became aware that we and our teacher friends might have discovered a way to frequently integrate creativity, mathematics, play, and literacy in intentional classroom instruction for children in pre-K–3.

We often heard how teachers struggle to find the mathematics in storybooks in which there are no numbers in the story, pictures of mathematical shapes, or mathematics vocabulary. When teaching a particular concept, they looked for a storybook with a context around that concept, such as money, addition, counting, and so forth. Although there are many web sites and books (e.g., http://www.living math.net/Home/tabid/250/language/en-US/Default.aspx) that list storybooks specifically geared toward a mathematical concept (see the reference at the end of this book), we found teachers often did not have these storybooks available to them, did not have time to find the books in their school or at a local library, or did not have money to purchase the suggested books. The teachers expressed a lack of time to read and follow a suggested mathematics lesson created in different literature and mathematics books and web sites. They also noted their lack of confidence with being able to use a storybook effectively to connect mathematics and pose mathematical problems.

We want to help teachers learn how to pose problems that can enhance their students' mathematical knowledge and stimulate their intellects with any storybook. We asked teachers in our workshops to see how mathematics can be found all around them in their world. They began noting time on their watches, height of the tables, number of people in the room, grouping of people into sets of those who were wearing dress shoes and those who were wearing sneakers, and properties of the shape of the trapezoidal tables. We then asked them to think about the fact that if mathematics is all around them in their worlds, could mathematics be all around the characters in the story and their storybook world? Suddenly, there were immediate looks of astonishment on the teachers' faces when they started to think about mathematics in the story from this point of view. Surely, any character could be faced with a mathematics problem and any setting could involve some mathematical exploration. The teachers were amazed at how they had never thought about looking at mathematics from the context of the setting or the characters in a storybook. They began to think about how children's natural connection and attachment to the imaginary characters in a story could interest them in solving mathematical problems for these characters.

In our workshops, we share the fact that children up to approximately ages 7 or 8 years enjoy stories with imaginative characters and make-believe settings and tend to engage in play and fantasy to simulate the real world (Egan, 2005). Thus, by using storybooks, teachers are able to engage students' emotions and imagination in solving mathematical problems, and they do so as though they are a part of the story. The mathematics becomes real to the children, and they see the mathematics as part of everyday life, even in the make-believe world of the storybook. As one teacher shared with us, her kindergarten students used to groan when she told them it was mathematics time. Now that she incorporates the mathematics instruction with a storybook and has the children doing mathematics related to the story, they are more eager and excited to do the mathematics. She noted that they do not even realize they are having "math time" (Wilburne et al., 2007). Her hesitation to try the storybook approach to teaching mathematics was quickly abandoned when she saw how excited her students became to solve problems she posed from *Minnie's Diner: A Multiplying Menu* (Dodds,

2004). *"They were pretending they were asking one of the characters to figure out how many sandwiches would be on the waitress's plate if all the sons ate two sandwiches."* This teacher told us she would never have believed her eyes unless she had seen it herself.

The teachers found that when they could use any storybook and create mathematical problems, they were able to make the mathematics more authentic and real to the children. They started to frame a mathematics lesson and problem around a story rather than looking for a storybook that related to the mathematics they were teaching. For example, rather than looking for storybooks that talked about money, kindergarten teachers selected storybooks they felt would be interesting and developmentally appropriate for their students and had characters from the story face mathematical problems dealing with money.

Teachers expressed a sense of freedom when they realized they could enhance children's mathematical literacy with the resources they were already using for reading and writing literacy. Rather than wait for materials to be purchased or committees to approve resources, teachers felt free to simply ask the children in their class to pretend that all the animals in a story might come to the classroom tomorrow. With a free and playful spirit, teachers created problem-solving scenarios about families of ducklings, forest creatures, cowboys, jungle families, princesses, and more. As we listened to workshop participants' problem-solving scenarios, we could see that their students would be given a chance to practice thinking about measurement when the teacher asked them to figure out how much playground space would be needed if 10 or 20 ducklings came for a visit. Another group of participants designed a problem in which the students could practice representing data when the teachers explained that the principal asked for a report showing how many animals would be staying on the ground and how many would prefer to stay in the trees above the playground.

Many teachers of young children told us of their desire to find ways to increase the amount of time children engage in imaginative thinking during the classroom day. We often heard teacher gratitude for strategies that invite children to pretend with story characters and classmates in ways that connected to curricular goals in reading and mathematics.

Children are motivated and stimulated to solve mathematics problems when they are presented in the context of a storybook (Hong, 1996). Their ability to pretend and imagine enables them to become emotionally involved with the storybook and enter into the storybook world. In this world, the mathematics appears relevant and real, as opposed to when mathematics is taught through expository instruction (Seifert, 1993). Young children learn more effectively in settings that are familiar to them and when the learning is in a context that is meaningful for them (Althouse, 1994; Copple & Bredekamp, 2009; Good & Brophy, 1987). Because the goal in mathematics education is to engage students in mathematics and mathematical thinking, finding ways to make this type of thought meaningful is essential, whether it be through imaginative or real-life problems. The storybook worlds provide contexts that are familiar and interesting to children, thus making the mathematics more meaningful.

Storybook worlds also provide teachers with familiar, interesting, and meaningful contexts to pose problems. Many teachers reported that their enjoyment of storybook characters and contexts actually helped them begin to overcome their lack of confidence with higher level mathematical thinking. As teachers considered problems from the perspective of storybook animals, families, and children, the playfulness of their questions increased and the discomfort with the mathematics decreased. The freedom to wonder, propose, consider, and guess with story characters seemed to gradually provide the teacher, as well as the children, with awareness of the mathematics that is all around in their real worlds.

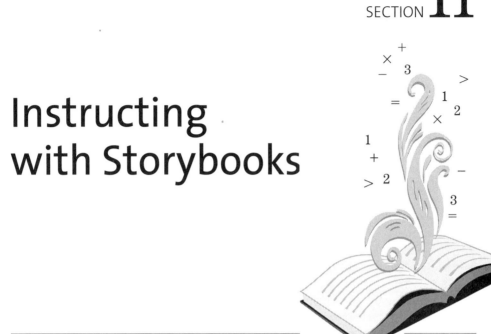

Instructing with Storybooks

nstructing literacy with storybooks is a traditional strategy for teachers of young children. Instructing mathematics with storybooks is a less traditional strategy. Engaging children in discussions before, during, and after reading storybooks is a time-honored activity for which teachers plan. Therefore, instructional routines have been established in most preschool and primary classrooms when children think together about a story and the characters. Although these discussions usually begin with a focus on ensuring comprehension of the story as written, many times children's questions and comments lead to discussions about topics far different from the author's written story. At other times, teachers pose questions that stimulate children's thoughts about new vocabulary, facts, concepts, possibilities, probabilities, problems, dilemmas, and more. Teachers in our workshops discovered that these discussions can include higher order thinking and mathematical problem solving with only a slight alteration of their instructional focus.

Three Approaches to Finding the Mathematics

As teachers took steps to make mathematical connections to storybooks, we found three different approaches that worked best. The first approach was to read through the book and find opportunities to pose mathematical questions. Then, teachers used a list of verbs associated with higher level thinking and the new Bloom's Taxonomy (Anderson & Krathwohl, 2001) as a guide to look for opportunities to pose higher level thinking questions that would require children to use their critical thinking and problem-solving skills (see Table II.1). We provide examples of the mathematics problems teachers first constructed with various

Table II.1.   List of verbs associated with higher level thinking

Analyze	Construct	Discover	Interpret
Choose	Create	Estimate	Imply
Classify	Deduce	Evaluate	Predict
Combine	Defend	Generalize	Propose
Compare and contrast	Design	Infer	Select

storybooks and then the higher level questions they constructed when they fo-cused on having children analyze, evaluate, and create. We also share examples of open-ended problems they created that required children to think and apply various strategies.

The second approach was to consider the different parts of a storybook and think about how different mathematical problems could be posed or how a math-ematical concept could be emphasized. We show how teachers looked at the plot, theme, setting, time frame, characters, objects, and illustrations of the story to find the mathematical connections. In addition, we share how teachers could pose a mathematical problem using each aspect of the storybook.

The third approach involved having teachers choose one of their state math-ematics standards or one of the NCTM Curriculum Focal Points (NCTM, 2006) and look for ways to connect the standard to the various elements of a story. Once teachers had a mathematical concept in mind around which they wanted to con-struct a problem, they found it was much easier to connect it to the storybook. With a little creativity, the teachers saw how any problem in their mathematics textbook could become a problem within the storybook.

In using any of the approaches, "teachers must be clear about the mathemat-ics they want their students to accomplish as they structure situations that are both problematic and attainable" (NCTM, 2000, p. 119). Each of these approaches is described in more detail in Chapters 5–7.

Once teachers became familiar with the different approaches to look for the mathematics in any storybook or how to connect any storybook to their curricu-lum standards, they were eager to design their mathematics instruction around these approaches. They began to recognize the need to integrate problems in con-texts to stimulate their students' interest and motivation to solve the problems. The level of playfulness became noticeable as the teachers laughed with one an-other as they generated imaginative scenarios that the storybook characters might encounter. They developed the disposition that they could create interest-ing and challenging problems to promote mathematical problem solving in their classrooms. Once they had success with posing problems, they began to see the richness of their students' mathematical thinking and the multiple ways their stu-dents were learning mathematics through problem solving. In a brief time period, they had become firm believers that problem solving needs to be emphasized in the pre-K–3 grades and that teachers need to be instrumental in finding the oppor-tunities to pose problems.

Let's examine ways in which a teacher can take any storybook and create mathematical problems and pose mathematical questions. All three approaches help teachers see how to capitalize on using storybooks to support, nurture, and extend children's mathematical thinking and reasoning. By looking at storybooks and using one of the three approaches, pre-K–3 teachers can be motivated to find the mathematics and gain confidence in their ability to do so. Teachers in our workshops found they could easily adapt storybooks to their mathematics curriculum and construct mathematical problems that were cognitively stimulating, authentic, fun, and exciting for their young learners.

The three approaches will help any teacher feel competent and confident in being able to integrate mathematics with storybooks. Throughout the book, we provide various examples of ways in which pre-K–3 grade-level teachers use these approaches to make mathematical connections and pose mathematical problems. There are endless numbers of storybooks that can be used and many different ways to integrate the mathematics. Our focus is on sharing these approaches with you to help you pose problems that will engage students in reasoning, critical thinking, and problem solving.

Student Interests

The first step in instructing with storybooks is to know your students and know how to present problems that will be interesting and engaging for them. Choosing storybooks with themes that relate to your students' interest will captivate their attention and help them easily relate to the mathematical problems. For example, students who are interested in sports or trains will find storybooks on these topics interesting and will become deeply engaged in making sense of the problems that are posed. Because young children develop their dispositions for mathematics from their early experiences, opportunities for learning should be positive and supportive (NCTM, 2000). Therefore, by designing mathematical discussions around topics in which children are interested, teachers are providing relevant and positive opportunities for children's mathematical learning.

Story First

The second step in instructing with storybooks is to begin by reading the storybook through once with children to focus on the elements of the story and to develop comprehension, which is one of the major goals of reading instruction. Young children rely on prior knowledge to interpret and construct meaning about what they listen to (Pressley & Hilden, 2002), and reading stories within a social setting enhances reading comprehension. Thus, when reading a storybook, students reap significant benefits by having discussions about what they read. When linking storybooks and mathematical thinking, students' reading and listening comprehension will also be positively affected. A shared reading experience typically enhances children's background knowledge, develops their sense of story structure, and familiarizes them with the language of books (Morrow, 1985; Morrow, Freitag, & Gambrell, 2009). Before reading storybooks, teachers invite students to predict what the story might be about, encourage them to focus on the illustrations and talk about what they see, ask them where the story takes place, and discuss the role of the characters and the plot of the story.

Linking Story with Mathematics

Next we suggest that teachers reread the storybook, focusing on engaging students in higher order thinking and mathematical problem solving as described in the next sections. Plan to revisit the storybook often to focus children's attention on different elements of the story and various concepts in mathematics. Repeated readings or revisiting parts of the storybook will help increase students' understanding of the story and simultaneously stimulate their growth in mathematics (Schiro, 1997).

Linking Other Books with Mathematics

It is important to help students make mathematical connections to the real world. Our final chapter, Chapter 8, provides ideas on how teachers can pose mathematical problems from books other than storybooks. Informational texts can set the stage for mathematical explorations and problem solving. Informational children's books, news articles, magazines, weekly readers, and textbooks, to name a few, can be used to create mathematical problems using the main concept, illustrations, or components of the text.

Chapters 5–8 include examples of lessons created by pre-K and primary classroom teachers. These examples are provided to stimulate teacher creativity in order to find the mathematics in the storybooks read to children. Examples for each grade level using each of the three approaches are presented and can be easily adapted to children of another age group.

CHAPTER 5

Posing Higher Level Thinking Questions

 critical component of teaching children mathematics is stimulating their thinking and engaging them in reasoning and problem solving. Our first approach deals with how to use storybooks to pose higher level thinking questions. Research shows that when teachers pose higher order questions, levels of student achievement are higher (Darling-Hammond, 1996).

As a pre-K–3 teacher, it is important to know how to pose questions that will require children to think. Questions such as "How many pencils are on the table?" "What shape is this figure?" or "What is the problem asking us to find?" require responses that simply answer the question. The teacher has a particular response in mind that they want the students to recite. Although these often are necessary questions to assess children's knowledge, they are lower level questions that lack the ability to stimulate children's thinking. Higher level thinking questions require children to have an understanding of the mathematics and knowledge beyond just applying algorithmic procedures. They may be questions such as "Why do you think the answer is five?" "How did you decide what strategy to use?" or "What does the answer mean?" that require students to think and explain their answers. Higher level thinking questions tend to be open-ended and have more than one right answer. Children need to be exposed to these higher level questions in order to develop their reasoning skills and to help them make sense of their own thinking. As teachers learn the value of constructing higher level questions, they will begin to see how to scaffold the class discussions and increase the opportunities to listen to their children's thinking.

This chapter presents strategies used in a professional development workshop to help teachers understand the difference between higher and lower level thinking mathematical questions and how to construct higher level questions from a storybook. We also look at how we worked with teachers to help them construct open-ended mathematics problems to encourage their students to think and use problem-solving skills. The chapter also shares samples of questions and problems teachers constructed at the workshops.

After our workshop discussions of lower order and higher order thinking, many teachers noted that they primarily ask lower level questions when they want to know what children have comprehended after a read aloud. In other words, they recognized that the questions asked called upon the children to engage in the lower order thinking processes of recalling and/or understanding. During our workshops, teachers practiced generating higher order questions related to the characters, contexts, and objects in the story. Each pair of teachers posed questions requiring skills of applying, analyzing, evaluating, and creating. What pleased teachers the most was the fact that they could skillfully integrate both types of questions before, during, and after reading any storybook. With a bit of practice, teachers blended "What happened next?"(remembering) with "Why do you think that was not a good idea?" (evaluating). We were gratified to read emails after the workshop indicating that the teachers recognized that posing higher order problems was no more difficult that posing lower order questions once they had practiced a bit.

Teachers commented on how often they asked questions to prompt children's recall of facts. One second-grade teacher stated, "*One of the facts is often about the number of items or persons in the story, but I never thought to place that question within a pretend scenario that might stretch the children's mathematical problem-solving thought processes.*" She recognized that her read-aloud comprehension questions sometimes touched on mathematical concepts but did not intentionally focus on thoughtful problem solving with number concepts. After reviewing the content strands of mathematics: number, operations, measurement, geometry, algebra, and data analysis, many teachers laughed uneasily and reported that they rarely addressed categories beyond number.

In our workshops, we provided a selection of questions to groups of teachers and asked them to separate the questions into two piles. Questions varied from things such as "Find the difference between 56 and 34," "Show three ways to represent 34 with base 10 blocks," and "Explain why the sum of two even numbers is even." As we walked around the room, we asked the groups what rule they used to separate the questions. In almost all cases, the teachers had separated the questions into the two intended piles that they explained were lower level and higher level types of questions. We then discussed what they considered to be the criteria for lower level and higher level questions. They identified the following criteria for lower level questions:

- Closed questions require one correct answer.

- Information is obvious and needs to be identified.

- Memorization or procedural thinking skills are needed to solve them.

Criteria for higher level questions included the following:

- Open-ended questions often have more than one correct answer.

- Information needs to be analyzed to determine what is relevant.

- Application of strategies is needed to solve the problem.

- Critical thinking or creative thinking skills must be applied.

The discussions often sparked comments such as *"I need to pose more higher level questions"* or *"Now I can see the difference between a lower level and higher level question."* Many of the teachers commented on how the higher level thinking questions related to the verbs used in the upper levels of Bloom's Taxonomy (Anderson & Krathwohl, 2001). We discussed the taxonomy and shared a list of the various verbs associated with lower level and higher levels of thinking (see Table II.1 in Section II). We provided this list of verbs and sample questions to guide teachers in constructing higher level questions to prompt students' thinking.

Our workshop goal was to have teachers construct higher level thinking mathematical questions around the content of a storybook. We modeled the process by reading a storybook and asking them what mathematical questions they would pose. We then asked them to look at the criteria listed for higher level thinking questions and the verbs related to the higher levels of Bloom's Taxonomy and work in pairs to construct questions. As the teachers shared their questions with the whole group, they were amazed to see how creative and challenging the questions were and how they addressed various mathematics concepts.

After we modeled the process, we asked teachers to select a storybook from a cart and read the story with a partner. Then, we asked them to make a list of the lower level and higher level thinking questions they could pose. Many of the pre-K–3 teachers found it easy to create lower level questions. They struggled at first with constructing questions that would require students to think and understand. After seeing samples of various higher level questions and having time to practice writing questions, they eventually expressed confidence in showing they could construct questions that would engage students' minds in mathematical thinking.

We also wanted to share with teachers how to construct problem-solving activities that would engage students in mathematical thinking, require them to use various strategies, and connect mathematical concepts. Most of the teachers were familiar with simple story problems that are often posed in mathematics texts that typically require students to apply an arithmetic operation. However, most of these arithmetic-type problems do not relate to students' everyday lives and do not engage them personally in the mathematics. To engage students in meaningful problem solving, the context of the problem needs to be complex enough to engage students' interests and thinking processes (Schiro, 1997). Our goal was to help pre-K–3 teachers construct problems that required thought and that had no set procedure to solve. We wanted the problem-solving activities to be such that the children could use various strategies to solve them and that there could be more than one correct answer. We emphasized that it is important to engage students in problem-solving activities to help them focus on the processes they use as opposed to just applying the mechanics of an operation to find an answer. Most importantly, we wanted the problems to be relevant to the children. We wanted teachers to see a difference between a story problem and a problem-solving activity. For example, a simple story problem might be as follows: *"Marc had three goldfish and Sandeep had seven goldfish. How many more goldfish did Sandeep have than Marc?"*

A problem-solving activity based on the same problem could be as follows:

How many of you have goldfish at home? What colors are the goldfish? How many of you have seen a fish tank with goldfish in it? Remember the story we just read Alexander and the Terrible, Horrible, No Good, Very Bad Day *(Viorst, 1972)? Suppose Alexander has a fish tank at his home and he has a total of 10 goldfish; some of them are orange and some of them are yellow. He has promised to write a story about his fish for his teacher, but he doesn't remember how many are orange and how many are yellow. Maybe he wants to know if we can figure out how many orange and how many yellow goldfish he has. What could be some ways we could figure this out if we can't see his fish tank?*

Solicit some responses. *"Let's see if we can figure out how many of each type of fish he could have."*

The problem-solving activity requires more understanding and strategic thought to solve the problem. Children may use strategies such as guess and check, draw pictures, use counters, or make a table. There is no one way to solve the problem, allowing students to be creative with their solution strategies. It is important to have children explain or share their solutions with other children in the class to model various ways the problem can be solved. Providing problems such as these and explicitly demonstrating ways the children can solve such problems will help them learn how to select and apply strategies appropriately.

Also, the problem is more relevant to the children. Connecting the problem to Alexander's world in *Alexander and the Terrible, Horrible, No Good, Very Bad Day* (Viorst, 1972) motivates the children to want to solve the problem for Alexander. They become more personally involved with the mathematics, even though it is posed through the fantasy world of the storybook. Providing rich, problem-solving activities such as this in the classroom actively engages students' minds and promotes mathematical inquiry and critical thinking. These skills will benefit children in upper level grades and in solving problems beyond the typical problems found in mathematics textbooks.

The following are sample lower level and higher level questions and problem-solving activities teachers constructed from storybooks using this approach during our workshops. In most cases, the teachers constructed the lower level questions first. Then, when they were asked to consider the criteria for higher level questions and look at the verbs associated with the analysis, evaluation, and creation categories of Bloom's Taxonomy, they were able to construct the higher level questions.

LESSON PLAN: Prekindergarten Example

BOOK: Kitamura, S. (1986). *When sheep cannot sleep: The counting book.* New York: Farrar, Straus & Giroux. (Jacket design from *When Sheep Cannot Sleep: The Counting Book* by Satoshi Kitamura. Copyright © 1986 by Satoshi Kitamura. Reprinted by permission of Farrar, Straus & Giroux, LLC.)

SYNOPSIS: When Woolly Sheep suffers from insomnia, he goes for a walk and sees many things. The book pictures many animals for children to count.

LESSON QUESTIONS

1. Lower Level Thinking Questions

How many bats did Woolly Sheep see? How many different things did he count? How did he get all those apples? How many times did he move the ladder?

2.   Higher Level Thinking Questions

How many living things did Woolly Sheep see that night? I wonder how many things he counted that were not living. When he saw all those doors and all those windows that night, do you think he noticed if they were all the same size?

3.   Problem-Solving Activities

a.   Let's pretend that Woolly Sheep invited all the animals he met to come for a party at his house, and all accepted his invitation. Of course, his mother would want to know how many animals were coming. Let's help Woolly Sheep figure out how many animals he had invited.

b.   Woolly Sheep's mother might ask if all of the animals lived on the ground or if some of the animals lived in the air and would need space above the table. Let's help Woolly Sheep make a chart for his mother showing how many animals would be on the ground and how many would be in the air above the table at the party.

c.   When Woolly Sheep looked at all the pictures he drew during the night, he decided he would like to decorate one wall with his pictures for the party. His mother wondered how much space he would need to hang all his pictures on the wall. Are all his pictures the same shape and size? How big do you think each picture might be? How much space would he need between the pictures? How could we use paper, scissors, and tape to help him figure out how much space he will need to hang the pictures?

LESSON PLAN: Kindergarten Example

BOOK: Allen, P. (1996). *Who sank the boat?* New York: Putnam Publishing Group. (*Who Sank the Boat?* by Pamela Allen. Used by permission of Penguin Group (USA) Inc. All rights reserved.)

SYNOPSIS: Five friends—a donkey, a cow, a sheep, a pig, and a mouse—all decide to go for a boat ride. They enter the boat from biggest to smallest, with each new entrant tipping the boat and causing it to sit lower and lower in the water.

LESSON QUESTIONS

1.   Lower Level Thinking Questions

How many animals were standing on the dock in the beginning? How many animals want to get into the boat? Why do you think the animals wanted to get into the boat? How might each animal help someone on the other shore? Estimate how many animals will fit into the boat. What do you think would happen if the first two or three animals sat on the same side of the boat? As each animal climbed into the boat, what happened to the number of animals standing on the dock? Do you think they were happy to wait, or were they sad to have to wait?

2.   Higher Level Thinking Questions

Did the shape of the animals cause the boat to sink? Do you think that the number of legs in the boat caused it to sink? Did the length, height, and weight of the animals cause the boat to sink? Did the shape or size of the boat cause it to sink? If all those animals climbed into the boat in a different order, would the result be different or the same? What do you need to know to figure out the answer? Is there some way we could figure out why the boat would float with some of the animals but not float with all the animals?

3.   Problem-Solving Activity

What if each animal had a very good reason to get to the other side of the lake? Let's pretend that the cow needs to give some milk to a baby calf who is hungry and crying. What if we were all there by the side of the boat—what could we suggest so that all the animals could get to the other shore? What if the animals would only do what we suggest if we tell them why the boat sank the first time—what would we tell them? What if we had a toy boat, a big tub of water, and a lot of toy animals—how could we show them what caused the boat to sink? Let's write a number story on paper to tell them, too.

LESSON PLAN: First-Grade Example

BOOK: Moore, I. (1991). *Six-Dinner Sid.* New York: Simon & Schuster Children's Books.

SYNOPSIS: Sid is a cat who is addicted to having six meals a day and glories in this life-style. Manipulative, persuasive, and a charmer, he has wrapped everybody around his little paw. Each owner believes that Sid belongs to them only . . . until the day he is found out!

LESSON QUESTIONS

1.   Lower Level Thinking Questions

How many houses did Sid visit? How many types of food did Sid eat at each house? Let's add all the types of food he ate in one day. Now, let's add up all the types of food the people did not eat when Sid was eating at each house. Let's make a number book that shows each meal that Sid ate on Aristotle Street. In the book, let's draw a map of Sid's neighborhood.

2.   Higher Level Thinking Questions

One family decided to take Sid to a veterinarian to help Sid eat only one meal a day. The animal doctor suggested that each family give Sid 20 tablespoon-size bites of food each day. Let's pretend that one neighbor offered to buy all the food for all the neighbors from the grocery store each week. If each neighbor decides to feed Sid each day, how many bites of food will the neighborhood have to buy each week? What if this neighbor wants our class to make a chart to help him remember?

3.   Problem-Solving Activity

Let's pretend that one family decides to buy cat food at the store to see if Sid will like it when he eats at their house. The cat food comes in a can shaped like a cylinder. Let's help him figure out how many tablespoon-size bites are in the can of food. Let's estimate how many tablespoon-size bites there might be.

LESSON PLAN: First- or Second-Grade Example

BOOK: Auch, M. (2002). *The princess and the pizza.* New York: Holiday House. (Illustration copyright © 2002 by Herm Auch and Mary Jane Auch. All rights reserved. Reprinted by permission of Holiday House, Inc.)

SYNOPSIS: A fractured tale of a princess who competes with other princesses to become the prince's bride.

LESSON QUESTIONS

1. Lower Level Thinking Questions

Princess Paulina loved to wave to the townspeople with her princess wave. In the story when she waved, nobody waved back, so she decides to throw some kisses. If she throws one kiss every minute, how many kisses can she throw in ½ hour? How many kisses can she throw in 2 hours? If she throws two kisses every minute, how many kisses can she throw in ½ hour?

2. Higher Level Thinking Questions

Princess Paulina found her talent—making pizzas. Suppose she decides to use pepperoni, mushrooms, and onions on her pizzas. She wants to know how many different pizzas she can make if she puts one, two, or three toppings on the pizza. Let's try to help Princess Paulina figure this out.

3. Problem-Solving Activities

    a. Princess Paulina likes to make pizzas. If she likes to cut her pizzas into eight slices, how many pizzas does she need to make to feed 34 people? Let's say Princess Paulina made some pizzas for our class. How many pizzas would she need to make if we each wanted to eat two slices?

    b. Let's look at the picture of the bed Princess Paulina climbed on to sleep. How many mattresses do you see? In another room, there was another bed full of mattresses. Princess Paulina noticed that for every foot tall, there were three mattresses. Let's look at a yard stick to see what that means. If the bed was 104 inches tall, how many mattresses were on the bed?

LESSON PLAN: Second-Grade Example

BOOK: Aardema, V. (1992). *Bringing the rain to Kapiti Plain*. New York: Penguin Group. (*Bringing the Rain to Kapiti Plain* by Verna Aardema and illustrated by Beatriz Vidal. Used by permission of Penguin Group (USA) Inc. All rights reserved.)

Synopsis: A cumulative rhyme that describes the sequence of events in which one person engages to bring needed rain to the African plain.

LESSON QUESTIONS

1. Lower Level Thinking Questions

How many actions did the main character take to bring the rain? Which action did he do first? Second? Third? Last? Let's read the book again and add up all the unhappy things that happened before the rains came. Now, let's figure out how bad things stopped when the rain came. What other good things might happen because the rain came?

2. Higher Level Thinking Questions

How many animals lived on the plain? Therefore, how many animal eyes did the boy see? How many tails? How many hoofs? Paws? What if half the animals wandered away from the plain to a land where there was more water? How many animals would be left? What would happen on the plain if it rained first? What would happen if it rained so much that there were huge puddles at first and then ponds all over the plain? Do you think that the animals would stay? Do you think that some of the animals would leave? Which would go first? Last?

3.   Problem-Solving Activity

Let's pretend that our class took a trip to Africa to meet these animals—after the rains came. All the animals needed to be measured so the town's mayor would know if the drought had harmed the animals. Let's pretend that the boy needed to get all the animals measured, and he asked us to help him. Which animal do you think would be tallest? Shortest? Heaviest? Lightest? What tools would we need to measure each animal's height, weight, leg length, ear length, and tail length? Let's pretend that the mayor decided that the animals needed a barn to live in the next time that the sun beat down for many days at a time and no rain came. How long, tall, and wide would the barn need to be to give shelter to two of each animal?

LESSON PLAN: Third-Grade Example

BOOK: Friedman, A. (1994). *A cloak for the dreamer.* New York: Scholastic. (The cover of *A Cloak for the Dreamer*, by Aileen Friedman and illustrated by Kim Howard, appears courtesy of Scholastic Inc. Copyright © 1994. All rights reserved.)

SYNOPSIS: Once there was a tailor who had three fine sons. When the archduke ordered new clothes for an important journey, the tailor asked his sons for help. The father was pleased with Ivan's and Alex's work, but alas, although Misha's cloak of circles was very beautiful, it was full of open spaces.

LESSON QUESTIONS

1.   Lower Level Thinking Questions

Divide the class into three teams. Each team is asked to find and count all the examples of the shape assigned to them. What if the archduke wants to know the total number of shapes in all three capes. How could we find out without counting all over again? How many different kinds of triangles are in the capes? Why are there spaces in Misha's cape and not Ivan's and Alex's? How many corners do you think there are in Ivan's and Alex's capes? How many corners are in Misha's cape?

2.   Higher Level Thinking Questions

What if the archduke told the tailor that he did not want any rectangles on his clothes? What could Ivan and Alex do? How many triangles would there be on the capes if all the rectangles and squares were cut into triangles? Let's draw a cape with only triangles that would have no spaces between them. If the cape is 36 inches by 36 inches, how many triangles would be needed to fill the cape if each triangle had an area of 6 square inches? What do we need to know to figure this out?

3.   Problem-Solving Activity

The archduke is worried about his three capes. He is determined to look very handsome when he visits his friend in America. He thinks the shapes on all the capes are too big, so he asks that each shape be cut into four pieces. How many shapes are there now? How do we measure the shapes? How many shapes will there be when each shape has been cut? How big will each shape be when they have been cut?

CHAPTER 6

Using the Storybook Elements Approach

ne way to use storybooks to find mathematics and create interesting lessons and discussions is to consider the various elements of a story. By using the plot, characters, setting, or objects in a story, teachers can identify situations in which a mathematics problem may exist. Teachers can also rewrite part of a story to create mathematics problems using these elements. Using the storybook element framework (see Figure 6.1) as a guide, teachers have been successful connecting mathematical concepts and posing mathematical problems based on a storybook. We describe this process further and share examples of how teachers have created mathematical problems using the elements of a story as the context.

Using the Plot of a Story

The plot represents the series of events or what happens in a storybook and addresses the major problem that the main character faces or what the main character hopes to achieve. The plot in a story involves four parts: a conflict, a rising action, a climax, and a resolution. The conflict is a problem the main character of the story is facing. The rising action involves how the character deals with the problem. Often students relate to the main characters and are eager to help them solve the problem. The climax is the culmination of all the action in the story and the point where a solution to the problem may be reached. The resolution is the wrap-up of the story and usually describes how the character deals with finding the solution.

So let's look at how to find mathematics in the plot of the story. Many plots involve a sequence of actions that can promote activities.

1. Have students list the actions in the logical order to develop sequencing and order.

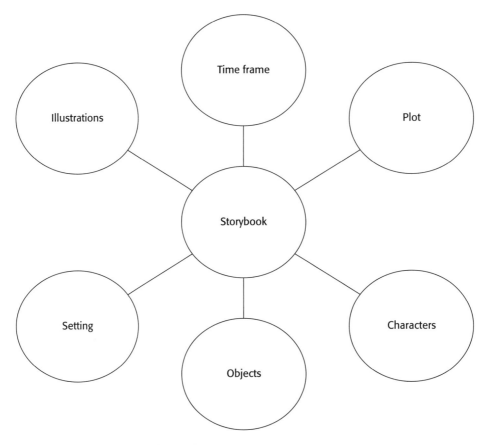

Figure 6.1.   The storybook element framework.

2.   Present clues to have students identify a part of the story.

3.   Compare actions that occurred at different events.

4.   Consider books with plots that lend themselves to a mathematical problem, such as *A Grain of Rice* (Pittman, 1986), which is a story about the growth of numbers.

5.   Look for plots for which students can predict what might happen next.

6.   Ask yourself questions such as "What can students learn by engaging with the plot?"

7.   Think about how you might redesign the plot to create a mathematical problem.

8.   Ask questions about the plot to connect to a mathematics concept.

9.   Have students explore conjectures, generalizations, or estimations based on the plot.

10.   Take a mathematical walk in the story and think about the plot from beginning to end. What other possible avenues or endings could the story have taken?

Let's look at an example of a mathematical problem using the plot of a story. In the storybook *Sergio Makes a Splash* (Rodriquez, 2008), Sergio is a penguin who loves water when it is in the form of baths and ice. When his class goes to the beach, he panics because he does not know how to swim and he is afraid to try. Eventually, he gets the courage to jump in and realizes how much he loves the beach water.

A first-grade classroom teacher placed four small bowls on a table in the classroom that was covered with a piece of fabric that had fish on it. She placed a small sign next to each bowl with a picture to represent the words *pool, lake, ocean,* and *swamp.* Life Saver candies were spread around the top of the table as well. The students were instructed to place a Life Saver candy in the bowl that represented where they liked to swim. Do they like to swim in a pool? Do they like to swim in a lake? Do they like to swim in the ocean? Or do they like to swim in a swamp? Each student took a turn to cast their vote. The Life Savers in each bowl were counted by students in the class, and the teacher had the students create a graph to show how many preferred to swim in each place. A larger version of the graph was made using the interactive whiteboard with students taking turns shading in the columns. The teacher posed questions to the class to help the children understand how to interpret the graph and determine where most of the students liked to swim and the location that was their least favorite place to swim. In this example, the plot of the story set the stage for the mathematical concept and lesson on creating and interpreting graphs.

Using the Characters in a Story

The characters in a story make the story real to children. The dilemmas characters face, their appearance, what they do in the story, or their personalities can help set the stage for an interesting mathematics problem. A farmer in a story can be wondering how she can plant 12 seeds in a rectangular array or how to fence in her cow farm with various-sized fence pieces. For example, if she has 3-foot and 4-foot sections of fencing, can she enclose a rectangular piece of land with a perimeter of 12 feet? (Yes, she would need to use four 3-foot sections). Could she enclose a rectangular piece of land that has a perimeter of 20 feet? (Yes, four 3-foot pieces and two 4-foot pieces). Granted, this is a challenging problem for a group of third graders, but it requires them to add combinations of four and three around a perimeter and to apply their problem-solving skills. There is no end to the number and type of problems this farmer could face.

One technique that has proven effective with teachers in creating mathematical connections is to make the characters come to life and pretend they enter the classroom. Think about taking a character out of the storybook and into the children's classroom, bedroom, kitchen, or community park. Only your imagination can limit where that character can go and what mathematical problems that character might face. As Vygotsky's (1978) research shows, children can often pretend to do what they cannot do in real life, and they can engage in higher level thinking and reasoning to solve complex problems. Children relate to the characters in stories and want to help the characters solve their problems. So although the character may be make-believe, the mathematical problems they encounter appear real to the children.

We found teachers were very creative and able to take any problem from a textbook, or problems related to their state standards, and have a character from a story be faced with the problem. For example, the following problem was found in a first-grade textbook: "Given the pattern A B A B B A B B B . . . , what letter will be in the 20th position?" In one first-grade teacher's classroom, she posed the problem around the popular storybook, *Diary of a Wombat* (French, 2003). In the book, the main character, Mothball, trains her human parents to know when she wants carrots and when she wants oats. The teacher told her students to suppose that Mothball liked to eat foods in a pattern. One day Mothball wanted to eat in the following pattern: oats, carrots, oats, oats, carrots, oats, oats, oats, carrots, and so forth. Mothball wanted to know if the children could help her figure out what would be the 20th food item she would eat if she continued this pattern. (As the teacher continued with the problem, she asked students how they could abbreviate the words to make a pattern. Students used the letter *O* to represent oats and *C* to represent carrots). By having Mothball faced with the problem, the first-grade students were overheard saying things like, "Well, next she would eat carrots, then she would eat the oats." The problem became real to them and they were motivated to help Mothball find her 20th food item. Basically, any character from any story could be faced with a similar problem; only your imagination can limit the types of items and the pattern to be solved.

When teachers say to children, "Let's pretend," suddenly, there is no limit to what the children can think. "Their imaginative and fantasizing capabilities are one of the most powerful parts of children's intellectual life" (Schiro, 2004, p. 77). Children love to play and imagine. By having children pretend that one of the storybook characters has entered their classroom and is sitting on the same classroom rug as them and has a problem he, she, or it needs them to help solve, they become enthusiastic mathematical problem solvers. In numerous pre-K–3 classrooms, we have seen how young children become quickly engaged and excited to solve problems to help these imaginary storybook characters. Teachers are amazed at how motivated the students are to do mathematics to help the characters. We also found how motivated the teachers became to create mathematical problems and how they began enjoying teaching mathematics. The pre-K–3 teachers found the problems were also more real to them when they had the storybook characters pose mathematical problems.

Creating mathematical problems for storybook characters takes a little practice. To help in this process, teachers might consider asking themselves the following questions:

• What can the characters say that could require students to engage in mathematical thinking?

• What situations can you create that would require the character(s) from the story to use mathematics?

• What open-ended tasks can characters face for which they need the children to help them solve?

Using the Illustrations in a Story

A story's illustrations can capture a child's interest and help him or her visualize the story. Students of all ages can enjoy the colorful and artistic pictures and imagine or fantasize being a part of the story. The illustrations provide opportunities for teachers to have students focus on the details in a picture or on the bigger, broader picture to connect mathematical ideas to the story. By posing questions about what students see in the illustrations and having students imagine various changes to the pictures, teachers can facilitate students' mathematical thinking. For example, in the background of a picture in a storybook about a farmer are a plump, jolly pig and a thin, sad-looking chicken. A first-grade teacher asked the students to compare and contrast what they saw in the picture of the pig and the chicken. Then, she asked the students to estimate the weights of the pig and chicken and that led to having students estimate their own weights. Later, students took turns getting on a scale to find out their actual weight and compared it with what they had estimated. The teacher helped them find the difference between their two measures and encouraged the students to use their base 10 blocks to be accurate in their computation. She made a list on a large sheet of poster paper and facilitated a discussion on the differences of the measurements.

Using any picture or illustration can be a starting point for a mathematical discussion on a concept in the curriculum. Pictures and illustrations help the students see mathematics in a more realistic context as opposed to a word problem like those often found in textbooks. Relating to the picture or illustration helps students identify with the realistic images that make the story come to life.

Using the Setting of a Story

Storybooks typically have many settings that appeal to young children. As a teacher reads a story, he or she can identify the setting in the story and look at how the setting relates to the students. For example, does the story take place in a character's home, a castle, or a faraway place? Does it take place in an urban, rural, or suburban area? What are the weather conditions in the story? In what geographical location does the story take place? Using the setting can have students focus on a house, a backyard, or a mysterious place in the story and can encourage them to think about various mathematical situations that could be possible. For example, a story that takes place in a character's backyard could offer ideas for mathematical data explorations and graphs comparing the number of trees in the storybook with the number of trees in the students' own yards or the number of pets in the story and the number of pets each child has. Some storybooks have multiple settings and can allow for a number of different mathematical topics. The story *Chaucer's First Winter* (Krensky, 2009) has Chaucer in a cave, on some icy hills, and in the woods. The woods have pine trees of all different sizes covered with snow. One teacher facilitated a discussion about how high pine trees grow each year and asked students to predict how old they thought the pine trees in the picture might be. Another teacher had students discuss the shape of snowballs, which led to an exploration of the properties of a sphere.

Different settings can also set the stage for different themes in mathematical corners or literacy circles. A story with a setting in a store can be the design for a shopping area in the mathematics corner with play money, items laminated with prices, and adding machines or calculators to compute the totals.

Using the Objects in a Story

Children as young as 1–2 years of age can identify familiar objects in a storybook (Giorgis & Glazer, 2009; Howes, 2003). As teachers read stories to children, they often point out the various objects on a page or have the children tell the class what objects they see. The objects may be something children find in their world and are familiar with, such as various types of flowers, toys, or pets. In some cases, the objects may be unfamiliar to the children, so talking about them provides a learning opportunity. The shape, characteristics, and use of objects can be topics for mathematical problems. Mathematics problems that require students to use basic operation facts are simple to pose. For example, a problem involving basic addition could be "How many tulips are on this page?" or "How many tulips are on these two pages all together?"

Characteristics of objects can be the context for problems in which students need to compare and contrast or put objects in various classifications of sets. In one case, a teacher showed her students a page of a storybook with various animals on it. She explained to the children that the mayor of the town needed to know how to put the animals into two groups to protect them from storm conditions during the winter. Of course, the mayor asked "our class" to help him figure out how to do this. In small groups, the children showed the mayor how they thought the animals should be grouped and also gave a rule for their grouping.

In another classroom, a teacher showed a picture of several ducks swimming in a pond. He asked the class if they had ever seen a pond. He then asked them what they could find in a pond. After they made their list, he asked them to make two columns and write down the living and the nonliving items under the appropriate column because the farmer's daughter wanted to send party invitations to all the living things in the pond. Later, the teacher helped them make an overlapping circle Venn diagram with the categories of *living* and *nonliving*, with *found in a pond* in the intersecting part. This is an example of a way to connect science with mathematics.

The shape of objects can also spark mathematical discussions. Comparisons of two- and three-dimensional shapes, irregular shapes, and shapes that may be convex or concave can be topics for mathematical discussion. In the storybook we spoke about before, *Chaucer's First Winter* (Krensky, 2009), the characters are shown building snowballs on one page. The spherical shape of snowballs led one teacher to a discussion on properties of the shape and how the shape is different from a circle and a cone. A hexagonal-shaped beehive in another storybook prompted a teacher to discuss the number of sides, vertices, and diagonals in a hexagon. Students then used various-shaped pattern blocks to create larger versions of the hexagon. They also looked at the tessellating property of hexagons and at pictures of floors with tiles that were in the shape of a hexagon.

Using Element Framework

As we worked with teachers, we encountered some hesitation on their part to pose mathematical problems using storybooks and engage their students in higher level thinking. They were not sure they could create their own problems. In some cases, teachers expressed how they used spiral curriculum programs that offered little opportunity to supplement with additional resources. They had not thought to integrate mathematics into storytime. Let's look at an example to see how to use this element framework with a storybook.

LESSON PLAN: Second-Grade Example

BOOK: Viorst, J. (1972). *Alexander and the terrible, horrible, no good, very bad day.* New York: Atheneum.

Alexander and the Terrible, Horrible, No Good, Very Bad Day

We took a storybook that was familiar to many teachers and looked at the elements framework to set the context for mathematics problems that could be posed. We started by describing the plot of the story and focused on the number of horrible events that happened in Alexander's life and looked at it as data the students could tally and graph.

Below are several other examples of ways in which mathematical problems could be posed throughout the story.

PLOT: Alexander has a day in which everything does not go well for him. The story is written so that students and adults can relate to his frustration and understand how there can be days like this.

How many things went bad for Alexander in the story? Make a tally chart with the number of terrible things that happened to Alexander. Let's pretend that Alexander wants to convince his dad that the whole family should consider moving to Australia, and he has decided that if he reports how many terrible things might happen to him in a week or year, his dad could be convinced to consider Australia, too. Further, let's pretend that Alexander is a friend of ours, and he has asked us to help him persuade his dad. If Alexander had the same number of terrible things happen to him every day for a week, how many terrible things would that be? Can we make a tally chart to show Alexander's dad?

SETTING: There are lots of different settings in this story where mathematical problems could be posed. Below is a list of some of the settings for this story and some examples of mathematical problems.

- Alexander's classroom

- Alexander's car

- Dad's office

- Shoe store

- Dentist's office

- Australia

Mathematical Problems Using Australia as the Setting

I wonder what Alexander's fascination with Australia is? How far do you think Australia is from where Alexander lives now? How do you think we could find out? If he had his own airplane and flew to Australia, how many hours do you think it would take? Let's make a table of our estimated number of hours and miles and compare them with what we find out when we research the questions. Let's look at a map of the world with the scale that represents mileage. If Alexander lives in our city, can we determine how far it is to Australia using the map?

Mathematical Problems Using the Car as the Setting

How many windows are in Alexander's car? If there are four children in the car and one driver, does Alexander always have to be smushed in the middle? Let's give Mrs. Gibson some suggestions regarding how to make it fair so Alexander doesn't always have to be in the middle. Can you draw the inside of a car and show how many different ways the four children could be seated in the car?

(This involves the concept of *permutations* and allows students to display information in an organized fashion.)

CHARACTERS: There are many members of Alexander's family in the book, along with some of his friends. Some characters include the following:

- Alexander
- Philip Parker
- His mother
- His dad
- His brothers, Nick and Anthony

Mathematical Problems Using Characters

Do you think that Alexander's teacher is a kind person who would help Alexander make a very good, wonderful day if possible? Let's pretend that Alexander wakes up the next morning and decides to tell about his no good, very bad day so that his teacher can help him have a good day at school. Of course, it would take him a long time to explain all the bad things that happened, so maybe Alexander and his brothers decide to tell about it in a number story. We could help them figure out how to do this, right? What would we need to do first? Second? Third? What would our number story look like?

OBJECTS: Let's look at some objects in the story.

- Sandwiches
- Shoes
- Books on desk
- Cupcakes in lunch

Mathematical Problems Using Objects

Philip's mother put a package with two cupcakes in his lunch. Alexander's mother packed no dessert in his lunch. How could Philip share his dessert with Alexander? What if Albert also wanted some cupcake; how could Philip share his two cupcakes among three people? What if Paul also wanted some cupcake; how could Philip share his two cupcakes among four people? Let's use our fraction pieces to show Philip how he could do this. Write number sentences to show the different ways to share the cupcakes.

ILLUSTRATIONS

Mathematical Problems Using Illustrations

The copying machine at Alexander's dad's office has lots of papers coming out of it. What could Alexander tell his father about these papers? Do you think the papers are rectangles or parallelograms? Why do you think that? What other shapes do you see? Let's draw these shapes on our dot paper and represent these shapes with our pattern blocks (e.g., rectangles, parallelograms, rhombus, square, trapezoid). Can we help Alexander describe different properties for each of these shapes? Let's make a list of the properties we find. What if Alexander were to walk into our classroom; what shapes would he find here? Let's make a list. What if Alexander were to go home with you today after school; what shapes would he find in your house? Make a list of the different shapes and what they look like in your house for homework tonight.

TIME FRAME: The time frame is 1 day in Alexander's life.

Mathematical Problems Using Time Frame

Talk about the routine of a day and how the pattern repeats. Create a Möbius strip to show the repetition. Organize the tally chart with the number of terrible things that happen at different times of the day, and make a bar graph to represent the total number of terrible things that occur in the morning, afternoon, and evening. Which part of Alexander's day was best? Which part of his day was worse for him? Let's look at the number of terrible things that happened in the morning, afternoon, and evening and find the mean number of events.

LESSON PLAN: First-Grade Example

BOOK: Krensky, S. (2009). *Chaucer's first winter*. New York: Simon & Schuster Books for Young Readers.

Chaucer's First Winter

TIME FRAME

1. Make a graph of Chaucer's day/year. How many hours/days is he sleeping? What if Chaucer asks the students in your class how many hours they sleep every day/night? How could we find out?

2. Mark a Möbius strip with the seasons: winter, spring, summer, and fall. This shows how the seasons repeat consistently every year.

3. Using a calendar, show how the months connect and the year progresses.

4. Discuss the concept of elapsed time.

    a. Time intervals used to describe sleeping for bears is measured in months.

    b. Time intervals used to describe sleeping for people is measured in hours.

    c. A home assignment could be to have children ask their parents how many hours they slept when they were babies.

5. Make a graph of sleep hours: baby, children your age, mom and dad.

6. Ask the question, *"If Chaucer goes to sleep in March, how long do you think he will sleep? When do you think he will wake up?"*

CHARACTERS: Chaucer says that his snowball is heavier that Kitt's, and Kitt says his is heavier than Nugget's. Whose snowball is the heaviest? How do you know? How could they find out?

Mathematical Problems Using Characters

The three animals decide to build an igloo. Kitt says that they need to measure the height of each animal. Kitt says that they need to know the height of the animals so they can make the igloo tall enough. They find some icicles with which to measure. Let's pretend that these pencils are icicles. (The teacher pulls some pencils out for students to use to measure.) First the animals want to measure Chaucer (an illustration in the book). If Chaucer were in our room, how tall would he be? Remember, he is a baby bear. (The teacher and children could look up how tall a typical baby bear is and then show the size on the wall. The teacher and children could do the same with Kitt, Nugget, and Daddy Bear, too.)

Storybook Element Approach Sample Lessons

This section of the chapter is designed to provide teachers with multiple examples of ways that a teacher might use the storybook elements approach with children. A sample lesson plan for pre-K–3 is included. Each sample lesson plan includes specific scenarios, questions, and activities that a teacher might use or adapt after reading the related storybook. A sample form for use in the classroom can be found in Appendix 6.A at the end of this chapter.

LESSON PLAN: Prekindergarten Example

BOOK: Waddell, M. (1992). *Owl babies*. Cambridge, MA: Candlewick. (Cover art reproduced by permission.)

SYNOPSIS: Three young owls are waiting on a branch for their mother to return to their tree home. As they wait, they think and talk together about what their mother might be doing and when she might come back. Each little owl expresses a different level of concern. When their mother swoops back to the nest, all three little owls celebrate with much flapping, bouncing, and dancing.

MATERIALS: Pine cones, acorns, markers, paint sticks, paper wings

STORY ELEMENTS

CHARACTERS: Three young owls

SETTING: Owl nest in a forest

TIME FRAME: Night time

PLOT: When will Mother Owl return?

OBJECTS: Branches and leaves

ILLUSTRATIONS: Night in a forest with three feathered owlets

Mathematical Problem Posing with Characters

Teacher: *"These three little owls all woke up at the same time and discovered a surprise, didn't they? I wonder why Sarah Owl was not as worried as Percy Owl."* In the discussion, the teacher might look for mathematics terms such as *older, younger, taller, shorter.*

We know that the mother owl was probably flying off to gather food for herself and for her little owlets, right? I wonder if Sarah Owl could have explained to little Bill Owl why she was quite sure that Mother Owl would return soon.

The discussion might lead to a talk about the fact that Sarah had lived more days and nights than Percy or Bill, so she might have had more practice in seeing Mother Owl fly off and return with food.

Mathematical Problem Posing with Setting

When the story begins, all three little owls are inside the tree in a nest. This is probably a really safe place for owls to be during the day when they sleep a lot. How do you think Mother Owl figured out how big a hole in a tree she would need to fit the entire family? If the little owls grow bigger they all might need a bigger hole for their nest, right? What if Mother Owl asked us to come help her measure; how could we help?

The children would need to think about how to measure the space and also each owl that would need to fit into the space. Perhaps nonstandard measure items could be used such as pine cones or wings.

Mathematical Problem Posing with Time Frame

Did you notice that Sarah tells her brothers that Mother Owl will be back, and Percy reminds everyone that she will be back soon? What does soon *mean? When our moms say that something will happen soon, do they always mean the same amount of time? What do our moms say when something will not happen soon? Well, here at school, we teachers often say that something wonderful will happen, but not soon. Instead, we will have to wait a long time until we have our 100 Days party.*

A discussion could occur about terms that describe time. Some terms mean a specific time, such as *noon* or *7:00 o'clock.* Other terms do not mean a specific time, such as *soon, later,* and *someday.*

Mathematical Problem Posing with Plot

The little owls seem to grow more and more worried as they wait and wait for the return of their mother. Maybe we could help the little owls by telling them what people parents do when they must leave their children for a while. People children go to a day care center where they play with other children and kind teachers who take care of them. Mother Owl told me there are 10 owl families in the forest and they might all worry when their mothers go away for a while. Let's pretend that we have promised to design a night care center for little owls. What will we need to decide?

This one problem could engage the children in thinking about each of the story element categories:

CHARACTERS: How many little owls will come?

SETTING: How much space will be needed? What kind of space? Branches? Nests?

🕐 TIME FRAME: Nighttime only? Daytime, too?

🚲 OBJECTS: What type of play equipment? How many of each would be needed?

The children could draw the center on the whiteboard or on mural paper. Alternately, the children could construct the owl night care center out of playdough or clay.

Mathematical Problem Posing with Objects

Let's pretend that Mother Owl decides that her little owls will be happier if they have some things to play with while they wait. Because owls are usually awake during the night and sleep during the day, what kinds of play things do you think they would like to have in their nest? Pinecones to throw? Acorns to roll down the branches? The nest is already very crowded, and Mother Owl wonders how much more space they would need in their nest if each little owl had a bag with 2 pine cones and 10 acorns? I think we could help her figure this out. Look, I brought these pine cones and acorns for each of you so we can try to help Mother Owl decide what to do next.

Pairs of children could manipulate the objects, figure out how many objects they would need for the three young owls, place them in some kind of container, and measure length, width, and depth of object. Some children might wonder if the objects could be hung in a tree branch rather than be smushed into the nest.

Mathematical Problem Posing with Illustrations

Teacher: *"Did you notice the wings of Mother Owl? As I looked at her wings, I thought they were symmetrical. How could we find out if real owl wings are symmetrical?"* The children and teacher could talk about finding information in books from the library or from the computer.

Look, the wings of the owls in these picture are just like in the Owl Babies *book; they are symmetrical. What about Sarah, Percy, and Bill? Do you see symmetry in their wings? Do you think their wings will be symmetrical when they are grown-up owls? Listen, I think I just heard little Bill ask what symmetry is. How could you all show little Bill what symmetry is and how people children can make things that are symmetrical?*

The markers, paint sticks, and paper or cloth wing shapes emerge from the teacher's bag, and the children are invited to explore and try to make designs with symmetry.

LESSON PLAN: Kindergarten Example

BOOK: Zemach, K. (2003). *Just enough and not too much.* New York: Scholastic Press. (The cover of *Just Enough and Not Too Much*, by Kaethe Zemach, appears courtesy of Scholastic Press, a division of Scholastic Inc. Copyright © 2003. All rights reserved.)

SYNOPSIS: In the beginning, Simon enjoys his cozy little house and his few belongings. Then he wants more and begins to accumulate a great many of everything until he cannot enjoy his cozy little house and his belongings. Simon solves his problem by inviting all his friends to a wonderful party. When everyone leaves, Simon asks each person to take items home with him or her, and then Simon is happy again.

STORY ELEMENTS

🌱 CHARACTERS: Simon and friends

🌳 SETTING: Simon's cozy house

⏱ TIME FRAME: **Several months or years**

📓 PLOT: **Accumulating items and eliminating items**

🚲 OBJECTS: **Chairs, hats, toy animals**

🎨 ILLUSTRATIONS: **House uncluttered, house cluttered, party, house uncluttered**

Mathematical Problem Posing with Characters

Simon was fortunate to have just the right number of friends. What would he have done if he had half as many friends? I wonder what he would have done if all of us had come to his party. How could he have divided his things among us?

This discussion provides the children with opportunity to experience the need to answer several questions to figure out the solution to the original problem.

Mathematical Problem Posing with Setting

Simon told me that his grandfather heard about his problem and wanted to know if Simon had considered making the house bigger so that he could keep all his belongings. Simon asked me to ask you if you could figure out how to make a house bigger. Simon seems to think that there is only one way to make a house bigger, but maybe there is more than one way.

A discussion could occur with spatial relationship implications. Perhaps Simon had told you the size of the house and the size of the property. Perhaps Simon could simply add rooms on to the existing house. Perhaps Simon would need to build up on top of his present house. Perhaps the children could draw floor plans or room plans.

Mathematical Problem Posing with Time Frame

Guess what? I received a telephone call from the TV person who wondered how long it took for Simon to turn his cozy house into a crowded house. She wanted to know how many weeks and how many months. Simon said he added something every day for a while, but he did not know how long that was. I assured the TV person that you could help Simon figure this out. Of course, we might need to ask Simon some questions as we figure this out. Do you think we will need a calendar as we work on this problem? When we get the answer, do you want to talk to the TV person, or do you want to give the answer to Simon and let him talk to the TV person?

Again, the children have an opportunity to realize that solving a problem includes several steps. The teacher can select a date to start the discussion and determine the number of weeks or months since then.

Mathematical Problem Posing with Plot

Did you hear that a reporter and camera person from a television station are coming to Simon's house to report Simon's good idea on the evening news program? Simon told me that he is glad that TV people are coming with their cameras, but he is worried, too. The TV man asked Simon some questions that he could not answer. Of course, Simon knows that I have good friends who would be glad to help him out, so he asked me to ask you the questions. You see, the TV camera people have asked how he knew there would be enough chairs, hats, and toy animals so that each party guest could take home the same number of items.

A discussion of sets could occur. Also, a discussion could take place about how items can be an element of one set in one situation and also an element of another set in another situation. At first, a set of chairs, a set of hats, and a set of toy animals could be identified with the right number of items in each set. At the end of the party, each chair could be assigned to a party guest. Small groups of children could move manipulative items from one set to another.

Mathematical Problem Posing with Objects

Did you know that Simon called me last night? He told me his friends had surprised him and brought back all the items he had sent home with them. They said that now their houses were no longer cozy. Now, Simon has decided to give all his items to the hospital playroom where children have fun while they are getting better. But he said he needs our help again. He wants to arrange the items in boxes to send to the hospital. There are 20 items to put into boxes, and he can fit 4 items in each box. Can we help Simon figure out how many boxes he will need? What if he has boxes that can hold three items in each? How many boxes would he need?

Mathematical Problem Posing with Illustrations

Let's pretend that Simon invites each of us to come visit him for 3 days at his house. Which house would you want to visit? The one that is quiet and cozy like on the last page of the book, the one that is full of Simon's new items, or the one with all the people attending the party? How many days would Simon have visitors if we each visited separately? What if we visited him in pairs—then how many days would he have visitors?

LESSON PLAN: First-Grade Example

BOOK: Winnick, K.B. (2004). *The night of the fireflies*. Honesdale, PA: Boyds Mill Press. (Cover art reproduced by permission.)

SYNOPSIS: Miko and Toshio bring a lantern and join other children to see the firefly release in Japan. When the principal takes the lid off the box, many fireflies fly into the sky, filling the area with blinking, sparkling lights. Miko and Toshio catch several and place them in the lantern they brought. Miko decides to take the lantern home so that she can keep the fireflies for herself, but she falls and a few escape. Her brother suggests that she carry the lantern carefully all the way home, but then he convinces her to let them go. Finally Miko agrees that the fireflies are more beautiful when they are free. The book concludes with an explanation of the firefly tradition in Japan.

STORY ELEMENTS

CHARACTERS: Brother and sister Toshio and Miko

SETTING: Japan, in a park and in a woods

TIME FRAME: One night

PLOT: Miko observes fireflies being released and catches some to bring into her house, but eventually decides to release her fireflies to fly free.

OBJECTS: Fireflies, a lantern, trees in the woods

ILLUSTRATIONS: Night scenes before, during, and after the original firefly release and Miko's firefly release

Mathematical Problem Posing with Characters

Let's pretend it is the day before the Firefly Celebration in Japan. All the children are excited, and they all want to watch carefully as the fireflies leave the box. So maybe the children are arguing over who will sit closer to the principal. I am sure that we can determine how to help the children solve this.

The discussion could include thoughts of geometrical terms. If the principal were to sit in the center of a large space, the children might sit precisely the same distance away if they determine the radius. If the children have yarn or string, they might enact the scene and notice that there is a way so that all children are the same distance away from a person in the center. Measuring instruments would help make the point.

Mathematical Problem Posing with Settings

Our principal and I were talking about the Firefly Celebration that they have in Japan. Our principal wondered if the book tells us if fireflies prefer the woods or the city. How could we find out? Maybe the illustrations in the book give us some clues. Maybe we could find clues in other books, too. Do you think the Internet would have an answer to this question? Maybe we will find information in many places. How could we collect our information in one place?

Mathematical Problem Posing with Time Frame

Let's pretend that Miko and Toshio have waited an entire year, and now it is time for the Firefly Celebration again. Their mother has given each child a watch and said that they may stay at the celebration for 1 hour. She has also said that they must plan their trip before they leave, and they must agree on how they will arrange their time between three places: city park, forest of trees, and the bridge. Let's pretend that the children must tell their mother where they will be all through the hour. Let's help them figure out how many ways they could divide up their time. What do you think they will choose?

Mathematical Problem Posing with Plot

Let's pretend that our city decided to have a Firefly Celebration just like the one that Miko and Toshio attended. Would we want to catch some fireflies? Would we want to take them into our houses to keep all night? Do you think we would want to play with some fireflies for a while and then let them fly away? Which way do we think they are most beautiful—in our jar or in the sky? Maybe our town mayor asks an artist to paint a picture to hang in the school to show the beauty of fireflies. Let's pretend that the artist asks all the children to vote which way the fireflies are most beautiful: in a jar in a child's room at night or flying free in the sky. Let's pretend that the artist has asked us first graders to organize the voting process. What will we need to do first? Second? Third?

Mathematical Problem Posing with Objects

Guess who I just spoke with on my cell phone? Miko and Toshio! They said that they have decided to take lanterns to their grandmothers because they are sick and could not come to the celebration. How many fireflies do you think they should place in each lantern so that the lantern will light up well? How many fireflies will they need if they put 10 fireflies in each lantern? What if they decide to give a lantern to each grandfather as well as to each grandmother? How many lanterns might they need? How many fireflies should go in each lantern? Oh my, I just had a thought: What if each child in the town decides to prepare a lantern for a neighbor or grandparent? How many lanterns would be needed? How many fireflies?

Mathematical Problem Posing with Illustrations

Let's pretend that Miko's teacher cannot come to the Firefly Celebration, so he called Miko and her friends and asked them to tell him all about the special evening. Maybe he asked them to think about how many fireflies were in the box that the principal carries. We could help them estimate, couldn't we? It is really hard to count flying fireflies, though, right? I wonder if we could pretend that the illustrations accurately show the quantity of fireflies.

The children might count the number of fireflies on each page and then add the number for the total. Perhaps the children might think of subtracting the number of fireflies that Miko and Toshio place in their lantern. They might also write an e-mail to their teacher describing the firefly evening.

LESSON PLAN: Second-Grade Example

BOOK: Sams, C.R., II, & Stoick, J. (2004). *Lost in the woods: A photographic fantasy.* Carl R. Sams II Photography. (Cover art reproduced by permission.)

SYNOPSIS: When birds and animals find a fawn alone in the woods, some of them assume he is lost. Others want to help him. This is a story of patience and trust. Mother Doe has assured her fawn that she will return for him. Because he was born without a scent, being alone is what keeps him safe. If Mother Doe stayed with her fawn, she would draw predators to him before he is strong enough to run from harm. The fawn must wait until his legs have grown strong before he can travel with Mother Doe.

STORY ELEMENTS

CHARACTERS: Fawn, frogs, blackbird, mouse, chipmunk, cardinal, goslings, goose, tree frog, katydid, squirrel, dragonfly, turtle, owl, meadowlark, raccoon, chickadee, and Mother Deer

SETTING: Woods

TIME FRAME: A day in the woods

PLOT: A fawn considers advice from animals but follows his mother's advice

OBJECTS: Trees and grasses

ILLUSTRATIONS: Photographs of woods and each animal

Mathematical Problem Posing with Characters

Last week I talked with my friend at the zoo about this book. He said that he might sell the book in the zoo bookstore, but he would need more information first. He asked me to ask you to organize the advice givers into animals, birds, and insects. I said you could do that. Then he asked that we classify the advice givers by color. I said you could do that, too. How will we report what we find to my zookeeper friend?

Mathematical Problem Posing with Setting

Why does the fawn have those white spots on his back? The mother deer does not have those spots. Why are those spots sort of round? Do you think any little fawns are born with perfectly square spots? Why? Why not?

A discussion of camouflage could include how light is filtered through branches in ways that resemble spots of light on brown. "*Let's look to see if we can find any shapes on the bodies of the animals. Remember, we were talking about angles the other day. I wonder if we can find any angles on the animal bodies."*

Mathematical Problem Posing with Time Frame

Did you notice that when it is the right time, each animal learns a new skill? I was thinking that the same thing is true for each person, too. How could we show the fawn and the mother when people learn new skills? Let's make a long number line and mark when we learn these skills.

Mathematical Problem Posing with Plot

Yesterday I was talking about the fawn book we read with the teacher across the hall. She wants to read the book to her class, too. She asked me if you all would be able to classify the advice into several categories. I said that I thought you could. Let's read the book again, and you tell me some categories we might use.

Possible categories would be *bad idea* or *good idea*. More complex categories might include *impossible to do, dangerous to do, might work well,* and *important to do.*

Mathematical Problem Posing with Objects

At the end of the story, the fawn tells his mother that he is ready to go off and explore with her. Let's write some more of the story. Let's pretend that his mom shows him how to choose leaves and berries to eat. He becomes particularly fond of the leaves on a large bush. He likes them so much that he eats three quarters of the leaves. Who will draw on the whiteboard what that bush might look like before and after the little fawn had lunch there? Maybe later in the afternoon, he finds a fence with raspberries and leaves growing on it and he is hungry again. This time he only eats half the leaves and berries. Who will draw on the whiteboard what that fence looks like when he leaves? What do you think he will eat next?

Mathematical Problem Posing with Illustrations

Did you notice that the animals in the illustrations seem to be all different sizes? I wonder if we could organize them all by size. I have glued a photo and name of each animal on some construction paper cards. Let's pretend that Mother Deer asks us to show her a size chart so she can help little fawn learn the many words that describe size. How could we use these photos to give Mother Deer what she requested?

LESSON PLAN: Third-Grade Example

BOOK: Van Allsburg, C. (1990). *Just a dream.* Boston: Houghton Mifflin. (Cover art reproduced by permission.)

SYNOPSIS: Walter moves through his days without awareness of the health of planet earth. One night a collection of vivid dreams shows him the future and the need for people to take good care of the earth. When Walter awakens he alters his behavior and begins to take action to take care of his part of the earth. He picks up trash, carefully recycles, and asks for a tree for his birthday. That night his vivid dream shows him the future when people take good care of the earth.

MATERIALS: Chart paper, pencils, erasers

STORY ELEMENTS

🌿 CHARACTERS: Walter and Rose

🌳 SETTING: Walter's real home and his dreamed places

🕐 TIME FRAME: Walter's now and his dreamed future

📓 PLOT: What will the future be like?

🚲 OBJECTS: Walter's bed, Rose's tree, dreamed items

🎨 ILLUSTRATIONS: Contrasting futures

💗 THEME: People's actions may decide the future

Mathematical Problem Posing with Characters

Rose and Walter both were happy with their birthday trees. Walter wanted to know how many trees there would be in their yard if they planted a tree on each of their birthdays. He would like us to make a table to show how he could figure this out. Let's help Walter figure this out.

Mathematical Problem Posing with Setting

Walter had a dream that he traveled in his bed to many places. He wanted some children to help him check out 1,000 future places. If all of us join him and dream one place every night, do you think we could identify 1, 000 future places for Walter to visit by the end of the school year? How could we figure this out?

Mathematical Problem Posing with Time Frame

Walter's dreams took him into the future. I heard Walter's mom wondering what he would have seen if his dreams had taken him into the past. In imagination, we can go forward and backward in time. Rose told me that she wants to know how many years into the future Walter's last dream took him. How could we find out? Rose also told me she wants to know what we all would find if our dreams traveled us back the same number of years. How many things would be the same? How many things would be different? Maybe Walter would want to report this information in his book or in a newspaper article.

Mathematical Problem Posing with Plot

In my dream last night, Walter came to our classroom. He stood right here in front of my desk and said, "I want you to show me something—something important. I am trying to convince grown-ups about the importance of taking care of the earth. Everywhere I go, I see people just dropping paper on the ground—like I did before my dream. I told my dad that your whole class had read my book and that you might be willing to help me persuade people to take good care of the earth."

"I want to send an article to the newspaper about the problem of grown-ups littering paper everywhere—on highways, in buildings, and in parks. Would you please help me figure out how to show that if one person does some bad things for the environment and then does some good things, the world can become better? The newspaper editor said she wanted pictures, charts, and number sentences so that readers could see quickly the change that one person made. I don't know how to turn my story into a chart, and I haven't learned how to write number sentences yet. Can you help me?"

Mathematical Problem Posing with Objects

This is the third time we have read this book, and this is the third time I have dreamed that Walter has asked me to help him out. He is planning to write another article for the newspaper, and this time he wants to know what kinds of items schools recycle and how much of each item is recycled in each school. How could we find out the answers to his questions at our school? Before we actually find out, it might be fun to estimate answers to his questions. Then, we could compare what we thought was true with what is really happening. After we find out, how could we show him what our school is doing about recycling?

Mathematical Problem Posing with Illustrations

Let's look at this picture of the hotel on top of Mount Everest. Can you imagine how difficult it would be to wash the outside of all those windows on top of a mountain? Walter is sitting up in his bed looking at the hotel and wants us to help him figure out how many windows there are. Let's estimate how many windows you think there might be. (Teacher lists the estimates on the board.) *What might be some ways we could help him figure this out? How could we use our multiplication skills to help Walter count all the windows?*

Mathematical Problem Posing with Theme

Some teachers proposed that this book could lead to an ongoing project. For teachers who have a small fund or access to donated items, there may be the opportunity to offer each child several pine tree seedlings. Perhaps these could be cared for and watered in the classroom for several weeks and then planted on the school grounds, in a park, and/or in the children's yards. The children might continue to revisit the project over time by an occasional rereading of the book, followed by further discussion of the theme of the environment. Problems to be posed might include the following:

PLOT

After you plant your tree seedling, let's pretend that you get to choose three places to see in your dreams of the future. Let's all draw all three future places with one of our tree seedlings growing there. Also, let's plan to hang all our drawings out in the hallway. How can we figure out how much hall space we will need?

With some scaffolding, children will be guided to consider how many pictures there will be, the size of the drawings, and the amount of space between the drawings. They might also measure the hallway space.

CHARACTERS

Rose and Walter have estimated the height their oak tree will be when they are 100 years old. However, they have challenged us to find out the answer for ourselves. Then they want us to figure out the size of our trees when the trees are 100 years old. How can we do this? Will all our trees be about the same size?

SETTING

In my recent dream, Walter whispered which future scenario he disliked the most and he told me why. Let's pretend that he asked me if you agreed with him. How could I get an answer for him?

The teacher can guide the children to think in terms of prioritizing, drawing the answer on a secret ballot, collecting the ballots, counting the ballots, reporting the number of votes on a bar graph, and writing a narrative report to give Walter in the next dream conversation.

⏱ TIME FRAME

The parent–teacher association has asked that each of us write a letter to Walter to tell him how much space your tree seedlings are taking up now. Also, I promised that you would tell Walter how much space your tree seedlings would take up when they are 10 years old if they were all planted near one another in the park. By the way, how can we figure this out when the trees are not 10 years old yet and when they are planted near one another? There must be some way to figure this out.

The children can check on the computer or in a book the average diameter of a pine or elm or maple tree trunk after 10 years of growth. Then the children would need to figure out how many trees and add the diameters together. The children could write a narrative, picture, chart, and number story for Walter.

Storybook Element Approach

GRADE LEVEL: ☐ Pre-K ☐ K ☐ 1st ☐ 2nd ☐ 3rd

TITLE OF BOOK: _____
_____

AUTHOR: _____
_____

ILLUSTRATOR: _____
_____

SYNOPSIS: _____
_____

MATERIALS: _____
_____

STORY ELEMENTS:

CHARACTERS	
SETTING	
TIME FRAME	
PLOT	
OBJECTS	
ILLUSTRATIONS	

(continued)

MATHEMATICS PROBLEM POSING WITH CHARACTERS: _____

_____

_____

_____

_____

_____

MATHEMATICS PROBLEM POSING WITH SETTING: _____

_____

_____

_____

_____

_____

MATHEMATICS PROBLEM POSING WITH TIME FRAME: _____

_____

_____

_____

_____

_____

MATHEMATICS PROBLEM POSING WITH PLOT: _____

_____

_____

_____

_____

_____

MATHEMATICS PROBLEM POSING WITH OBJECTS: _____

_____

_____

_____

_____

_____

MATHEMATICS PROBLEM POSING WITH ILLUSTRATIONS: _____

_____

_____

_____

_____

CHAPTER 7

Targeting the Curriculum Focal Points

 n the curriculum standards approach, teachers select a mathematics standard for the grade level and read a storybook looking for opportunities to relate the story to the standard. Because each state has different standards, we use the Curriculum Focal Points (NCTM, 2006) because of their intent to identify essential mathematics concepts for each of the pre-K–8 grade levels.[*]

Start by selecting a storybook you would read for the literary component or one that interests the children. Read through the storybook to get acquainted with the context of the story, as well as the characters and the plot. Because most storybooks do not have visible mathematics, it may take some imagination and creativity to discover where mathematical problems can occur.

Next, select a mathematics standard or focal point (NCTM, 2006) from your curriculum that you want to teach through the storybook. Consult your district curriculum for further details regarding what students should know and ways they can demonstrate their understanding of the mathematics addressed in the standard or focal point.

Once you have the mathematics standard identified and know how you want your students to demonstrate their understanding, select a character from the storybook that can be faced with a mathematics problem around the content. Use your imagination to create a situation that the character is facing and a problem that the children can help solve. In some cases, it might be helpful to select a problem from a textbook or resource that you want to come alive through the character. Appendix 7.A provides a template for identifying and outlining curriculum focal points that can be used in your classroom. Let's look at an example.

---

[*]Curriculum focal points for prekindergarten through grade 8 mathematics: A quest for coherence by National Council of Teachers of Mathematics. Copyright 2006 by National Council of Teachers of Mathematics. Reproduced with permission of National Council of Teachers of Mathematics in the format Tradebook via Copyright Clearance Center.

63

Prekindergarten

re-K mathematics emphasizes vocabulary and relationships. Students begin to count objects with a one-to-one correspondence to the numeral name, determine which set has more items or less, and recognize numerals. Teachers need to provide lots of opportunities for children to count and match numbers of objects to the numeral. Shapes and spatial reasoning are important and can be emphasized with real-world objects in both two and three dimensions. Hands-on activities in which children begin to explore and create shapes such as triangles, squares, and circles are important. Also, children should begin to understand attributes of objects such as length, height, and weight to develop measurement skills.

Almost any storybook can be used to encourage pre-K children to think about these mathematical concepts and engage them in mathematical explorations. What is important for teachers is to let the mathematics flow from the storybook. Think about posing questions on any aspect of the story, the characters, the illustrations, the plot, objects in the story, and so forth. In preschool classrooms, storybooks can also be used to emphasize literacy concepts, such as dramatization, choral reading, sounds, and rhyming words.

Because pre-K children love to play in the imaginative world, they can be led to think about a story in the land of pretend. As a result, teachers can pose questions that begin with "What if" or "Let's pretend" to spark children's interest and have them think mathematically, even if the book is not one with numbers in it.

We saw how a preschool teacher used storybooks to engage children in mathematical thinking based on objects and characters in a story. *The Napping House* (Wood, 1984) is a cumulative tale about a snoring granny who is sleeping on a rainy afternoon. Gradually, various critters crawl on top of granny (e.g., a child, a dozing dog, a snoozing cat) as she sleeps. The story ends when a flea sets off a chain of events which results in a pile of characters and a broken bed.

In the discussion after reading this book, the preschool teacher posed questions that engaged children in counting the critters or number of legs on the bed each time, and asked questions related to the possible weights of each critter. She posed questions such as *"Which critter weighs more?" "Which critter weighs the least?" "How do you know?" "Granny wants us to tell her what size bed she would need to fit all the critters."* She invited the children to pretend each of the critters brought a friend on the bed and asked:

How many critters would be on the bed now? What if the bed was shaped like a triangle—can you draw a picture of the bed? How many sides would the bed have? Let's pretend the bed is 1 foot long, can you show me with your hands how long the bed would be? (This was followed up by comparing hand measures with a ruler to demonstrate length of a foot.) Can you find something around the classroom that would be longer than the bed? Can you find something in the classroom that would be shorter than the bed? How about something the same size as a bed?

The discussions continued with children talking about the size of their beds. She also focused on the concept of sequences and vocabulary such as which came first, next, and last.

LESSON PLAN: Prekindergarten Example

BOOK: Hest, A. (2009). *Little Chick*. Somerville, MA: Candlewick. (Text copyright © 2009 Amy Hest. Illustrations copyright © 2009 Anita Jeram. Reproduced by permission of the publisher, Candlewick Press, Somerville, MA.)

SYNOPSIS: The book comprises three short stories about a little chick. In the first story, he tries to patiently wait for a carrot he planted to grow. In the second story, he is trying to fly a kite. And in the third story, he is trying to reach for the stars. A wise old hen, Old-Auntie, gives Little Chick advice in each story. Although there is no mention of the word *count* in the story, many pretend opportunities can be created to engage preschool children in counting activities.

 NUMBER AND OPERATIONS: Developing an understanding of whole numbers, including concepts of correspondence, counting, cardinality, and comparison

MATERIALS: Magnetic counters

I like this story. I like it so much that I would like to pretend with Little Chick for a while. I hope you will pretend with me. Did you hear Little Chick's grandfather? I think I heard Grandfather Rooster ask Little Chick how strong his legs are now that he is 4 years old. Did you also hear Little Chick tell his grandfather that his legs are strong enough to hop all the way from the chicken house to the carrot field? Little Chick sounded very proud, didn't he? Grandfather

Rooster looked very surprised, didn't he? When Grandfather Rooster asked Little Chick how many hops are needed to go all that distance, Little Chick didn't know. Do you think we could help him find out how many hops are needed each time he goes from his house to his garden? I think there are lots of ways that Little Chick could figure this out. Let's help him. What might he do to find out the answer?

The teacher could guide children to see that Little Chick hopped to the garden and count each hop (one-to-one correspondence).

This time, let's pretend that Little Chick hurt his right leg on a stone, and he could not hop anymore that day. Maybe Grandfather Rooster asks Little Chick to estimate or predict the number of hops. I think I heard Little Chick say he didn't know how to estimate or predict. We could show him how, couldn't we? Let's show Little Chick right now. Let's pretend that Little Chick's house is here near the window and the carrot field is over there near the door. When we predict, we imagine how many hops are needed. We know that our prediction may not be just the right number, but it is likely to be close to the actual number. We could show Little Chick how to predict and also how to count (when his foot feels better). So, let's show Little Chick how to do this so he can give Grandfather Rooster an estimated answer today and a counted answer tomorrow. Each of you will get a turn to predict, and then you will get a turn to hop. I will write your predictions on the whiteboard. After you have all had a chance to hop, I will write the actual number of hops on the board. I wonder if Grandfather wants an estimated answer or an actual answer. Maybe Little Chick should ask him.

In the story, we saw how Little Chick hops to a carrot. Suppose he wants to know how many hops it takes to reach the carrot. Let's pretend the carrot is here in the front of the classroom and Little Chick is standing here in our classroom.

The teacher picks a random spot in the classroom. "*Can you predict how many hops it would take each of you to hop to the carrot? Let's make a list of our predictions.*" The teacher records children's estimates on the board and has the children see whether they can find the lowest estimate and the greatest estimate.

The teacher continues, "*Now, let's take turns hopping from this spot to the carrot and see how many hops it takes us.*" The teacher selects several students at a time to hop to the carrot. The teacher counts the number of hops for each student with the other students counting along.

Little Chick changed his mind and decided to take large steps instead of hops. What if we took large steps instead of hops? How many large steps do you think it would take you to reach the carrot at the front of the room from this spot here?

The teacher collects the students' predictions and posts them on the whiteboard, saying, "*Let's see if our predictions were close.*" The teacher has students start at the spot she selects as the starting point and take large steps to reach the carrot. She counts with them as they make each step. She posts the students' actual numbers on the whiteboard next to their predictions. As part of the class discussion, she engages students in a discussion regarding whether their predictions of the number of steps were more or less than what they actually counted.

"*How many large steps do you think it would take Old-Auntie to walk from here to the carrot? How could we find out?*" The teacher then pretends she is Old-Auntie and the students count how many large steps it takes her to walk to the carrot.

Little Chick was hopping around the garden, and all of a sudden, he saw a rabbit hiding in the bushes. The next thing he knew, the rabbit was hopping quickly from one bush to another. The rabbit took big hops. Can you hop like a rabbit? Can someone show us how a rabbit hops?

What if the rabbit started at the same spot we started at—how many hops do you think he would take to reach the carrot?

The teacher can engage students in a discussion of how the rabbit takes larger hops so he would take fewer hops than Little Chick.

Little Chick wants to place small rocks in a circle around the base of the carrot plant to keep the rabbit away. He wants us to tell him how many small rocks he will need. Let's pretend these counters are small rocks. I am going to put some counters on the board and have you tell me how many counters there are.

The teacher begins by putting one counter on the board and having students count out loud, "*One.*" Then she puts two counters on the board and students count, "*One, two.*" The teacher continues placing counters up to five and changes the way she places them on the board. One time she places four counters in two rows of two, and another time she places the four counters in a horizontal row. She continues having students try to say the number of counters followed by counting the counters to verify the amount.

"*What if Little Chick wanted to put five small rocks around the carrot? Can you count five counters to show me what* five *looks like?*" The students use their own counters to count out the number *five.* The number can change depending on the students' ability to count. "*Let's take our counters and make a circle out of them.*"

"*Little Chick finds eight small rocks to place around his carrot. Can you count out eight counters to show me what* eight *looks like?*" If the students are not able to count to eight, the teacher might just model this for the students.

"*Let's see how we could make a circle with the eight counters.*" The teacher arranges the magnetic counters in a circle on the whiteboard. "*Let's count the number of counters, and let's mark this counter* [top counter] *as our starting point so we know where we begin.*" The class counts with the teacher as she points to each counter and counts to eight. Several students are then selected to count the counters for the class to repeat the process. "*I wonder if we could make another shape with the eight counters. Does anyone want to come to the whiteboard and rearrange the counters to make another shape?*" The teacher selects a volunteer to rearrange the counters. "*Let's see if we could make a rectangle. We could put three counters across the top and three counters across the bottom and one counter on each side. There, we have a rectangle.*" It would be a 4x2 rectangle. "*Let's draw a rectangle in the air with our fingers.*" The teacher can create another rectangle with two counters on top and two on the bottom with four counters on each side to show a 2x4 rectangle.

MEASUREMENT: Identifying measurable attributes and comparing objects by using these attributes

MATERIALS: String, paper inchworms, pencils with no points

In the second story in the book, Little Chick is trying to fly a kite made out of a leaf. He has trouble getting the leaf to fly high in the sky.

"*Little Chick wants to fly his kite that is made from a leaf he found on the ground. Have any of you ever flown a kite?*" The teacher waits for the students' responses. "*How high do you think your kite was off the ground?*" Again, the teacher waits for responses.

The teacher shows a short and long piece of string to represent the different lengths of string Little Chick could have used. "*I have two pieces of string here. Let's mark this piece string A and the other piece string B. What do you notice about the strings?*" The teacher waits for responses. "*Which piece of string is longer?*" "*Which piece of string is shorter?*" "*Let's measure the length of strings. I have some paper inchworms. Let's see how many inchworms long each piece of string is."* The teacher has several students place the paper inchworms along the string to measure the strings.

"I have some pencils with no points. Let's measure the lengths of the strings using the pencils." The teacher has several students measure the strings with the pencils. The teacher records the lengths of the strings in terms of the inchworms and the pencils on the whiteboard. The class discusses the difference in the measurements. *"How long is string A when we measure it with the inchworms? How long is string A when we measure it with pencils?"* Discussion continues with string B and the teacher emphasizing vocabulary such as *more, less, shorter, longer, same,* and *different.*

In the third story, Little Chick is trying to reach up and touch the stars. *"Can you all pretend to reach up to touch the stars? How far away do you think the stars are up in the sky?"* The teacher waits for student responses. The teacher might want to discuss the distance from earth to the stars as an extension of the lesson. *"When Little Chick is stretching to reach the stars, does he get taller? When you reach up to try to touch the stars, are you growing taller? Let's try to find out."* The teacher then has students come to the whiteboard and marks their height against the board with their names. The students come to the whiteboard and stretch their hands and stand on their tiptoes to make themselves as tall as they can. The teacher marks their stretched height above the students' original height. *"Let's see how much taller you were when you stretched up to reach the sky."* The discussion focuses on vocabulary such as *taller, more, less, shorter,* and so forth.

GEOMETRY: Identifying shapes and describing spatial relationships

MATERIALS: String

I wonder what kind of shape Little Chick's garden is. How many of you have a garden at home? Can you tell us what shape your garden is? Let's use the string in front of you to make some shapes. I am going to draw a square up on the whiteboard, and I would like you to make a square with your string.

The teacher walks around to see that each student is able to make a square.

Let's suppose Little Chick hopped into our classroom and wanted to see all the squares we made. Then Little Chick wanted us to show him where there were other squares in our classroom. Can you find other squares in our classroom that we could show Little Chick?

The teacher will respond to the various items the students select to verify whether or not they are in the shape of a square.

I think we found a lot of squares in our classroom. Let's make a circle out of our string. I am going to make a circle on the whiteboard, and I would like you to make one out of your string.

The teacher checks to be sure each student correctly made a circle. *"If Little Chick entered our classroom, I think he would be so excited to see all our beautiful circles. If he wanted to see some other circles in our classroom, what could we show him?"* Again, the students select items in the classroom that are in the shape of a circle and the teacher verifies their responses and asks students how they know the shape is a circle.

Excellent work! I think you found all the squares and all the circles in our classroom. Now Little Chick wants to describe to Old-Auntie what a square looks like. What should he tell her? Can someone help Little Chick describe a square? Can someone help Little Chick describe a circle?

The teacher solicits responses for each shape from several students and poses questions to be sure the students understand the properties of a circle and square. One example could be asking whether the sides of the square are all the same length. How do the students know whether the sides are the same length? How could they find out? *"I think Little Chick would be very happy to know we have squares and circles all around us. Let's draw some squares and circles on our papers."*

LESSON PLAN: Prekindergarten Example

BOOK: Rodriguez, E. (2008). *Sergio makes a splash.* New York: Little, Brown. (Art © 2008 by Edel Rodriguez. Used by permission of Little, Brown Books for Young Readers.)

SYNOPSIS: Sergio is a little penguin who likes many things, especially water. He enjoys playing in water, relaxing in water, and drinking water. However, when his teacher tells the class that they will learn to swim, Sergio feels frightened. Sergio's teacher, Mrs. Waddle, helps him remember all the fun he has with water in other ways and suggests that swimming in water will be fun, too. Eventually, Sergio overcomes his fear by putting on a floatie and jumping into the ocean. To his surprise, he discovers that he likes swimming, too. But when his teacher says that next time they will all learn how to swim without their floaties, Sergio is not so sure.

NUMBER AND OPERATIONS: Developing an understanding of whole numbers, including concepts of correspondence, counting, cardinality, and comparison

MATERIALS: Cut-outs of floaties (optional)

I like Sergio! I like his friends, too. Did you notice how his friends tried to help him when he was afraid? Let's pretend that we heard his friends whisper that they wish they had floaties, too. Let's pretend that Sergio heard them and promised to bring a floatie to each friend the next day. Sergio is a very young penguin so he doesn't know how to figure out how many floaties to bring.

The teacher can help the children figure out several ways to find out how many penguins are Sergio's friends. For example, they can count the penguins when they are riding in the bus and when they are swimming in the ocean. The children might notice that on some pages there are five penguins and on some pages there are four penguins. What might that mean? Is one penguin hiding or swimming somewhere else? The children might notice that there are always five penguins on the bus going to the swimming place and going away from the swimming place. What might that mean? The teacher might help the children realize that they can decide how many floaties to bring by drawing a chart that shows five individual penguins and attach (with tape or Velcro) a predrawn floatie to the wing of each penguin. The teacher might also help the children count the number of penguins and count out the number of floaties.

GEOMETRY: Identifying shapes and describing spatial relationships

MATERIALS: Pictures of igloos, toy penguins or cutout pictures of penguins

Let's pretend that Sergio and his friends enjoyed swimming so much that they stayed in the cold water a long time. One day a big polar bear came down to the water to watch them swimming. He asked the little penguins if they would like to learn some fancy diving tricks. They all wondered if a big bear could do any fancy tricks, so the bear quickly showed them tricks for diving into the water and then diving under the water, spinning around in the water and then popping above the water again. Next, he showed them the fancy trick of climbing up to the top of an iceberg. Then he showed them how to slide all the way down into the water, under the water, and all the way to the bottom of the ocean. Let's pretend our penguins are playing Simon Says with the polar bear and penguins. Let's think of some more tricks for them to do.

With toy or cutout penguins, the children could show on a slate or flannel board how the penguins would move to accomplish each change of spatial location.

Let's pretend that while the penguins were playing, Mrs. Waddle and Mr. Polar Bear asked us to help build an igloo for everyone for when they get cold and tired. Let's pretend that they ask us to help them figure out how to make an igloo out of the ice shapes all around them. Mr. Polar Bear and Mrs. Waddle brought their ice-cutting and ice-lifting tools. They are ready to work, but they do not know how to find out what shapes to cut out of the ice, and they do not know how to pile the blocks of ice into the igloo shape. I am sure that we can help them figure this out. How can we help them?

The teacher might bring pictures of igloos, cutout shapes, and flannel boards or Velcro pads.

MEASUREMENT: Identifying measurable attributes and comparing objects by using these attributes

MATERIALS: Cutouts of penguins (optional)

I have been wondering why Sergio was afraid to learn to swim in the ocean. Is it possible that he thinks he is too small to swim in an ocean with big waves? Maybe Sergio whispers to Mrs. Waddle, the teacher, that he is afraid because he is not big enough to swim in the ocean. On the first page, we learn how big Sergio is. He is 1 foot tall and weighs 1 pound. Mrs. Waddle wants to know the height and weight of all the penguins on the page. How could she help Sergio find out the height and weight of his friends?

The children might suggest that the penguins stand near one another and see if their shoulders are the same height or their heads are at the same height. The teacher might ask what tools we use to measure the tallness or height of something or someone. Of course, the teacher might also ask what tools we use to measure the heaviness or weight of something or someone.

Do you think that Sergio might stop being afraid if he knew that all the penguins are about the same size and they are all swimming in the ocean very safely? What if Sergio still does not want to swim in the big ocean? Maybe he tells Mrs. Waddle that he wants to practice walking around in a pool before he tries swimming in the ocean. I think that I heard Mrs. Waddle say she thinks the pool is too deep for penguins to walk in. Sergio told me that he looked carefully at the pool near the school and he really thinks that it is just the right size for penguins to walk in. Let's help him figure out how deep the pool would need to be to fit the penguins.

Teachers should guide the children to consider whether the penguins would want the water to be over their heads or up to their beaks or at the top of their wings. Also, the teacher might use toy (or cutout) penguins and a deep tub of water to show how many inches deep the pool should be.

What tools could help Sergio find this out? But what if some of the penguins are different heights? Maybe some penguins are 2 feet high and some are 3 feet high and some are the same as Sergio, 1 foot high? What difference would that make when they climbed into the water?

Kindergarten

Kindergarten Curriculum Focal Points

- **Numbers and Operations:** Representing, comparing, and ordering whole numbers and joining and separating sets

- **Geometry:** Describing shapes and space

- **Measurement:** Ordering objects by measurable attributes

t the kindergarten level, the curriculum focuses on counting activities, creating and comparing sets, ordering numbers, and classifying objects into sets. Simple readiness activities for addition and subtraction and identifying and counting coins are emphasized as well. Simple concepts are taught. Students begin to understand measurement by learning that a measurement can be expressed as a number and objects can be compared by their height or weight. Geometry activities are designed to help students learn vocabulary and how to identify and describe simple two- and three-dimensional shapes.

One kindergarten teacher in our workshop planned a lesson around units of money that focused on enhancing her children's use of mathematical language. She integrated various storybooks into her reading block and developed mathematics centers using the books and mathematical manipulatives such as play money, counting bears, and number tiles. She read stories such as *A Chair for My Mother* by Vera Williams (1982) to embed mathematical language into storytime. Her children engaged in learning about the value of money as they connected to the characters and the language in the story. The teacher discovered that by becoming engaged in conversations about the story, her children also developed important processes of reasoning and explaining mathematical relationships. In short, the kindergarten children were enhancing their understanding of mathematics through communication.

LESSON PLAN: Kindergarten Example

BOOK: Chen, C.-Y. (2004). *Guji Guji*. La Jolla, CA: Kane/Miller. (Cover art reproduced by permission.)

SYNOPSIS: When a crocodile egg rolls into a duck nest, the emerging baby, Guji Guji, is raised by a mother duck and plays happily with brother and sister ducklings. One day some scary, snarling, creatures inform Guji Guji that he is not a duck but a misplaced crocodile. Also, the crocodiles insist that Guji Guji bring all the ducks to the crocodiles so that they might enjoy a meal of duck. Instead, Guji Guji thinks and thinks and figures out a way to save his duck family.

NUMBERS AND OPERATIONS: Representing, comparing, and ordering whole numbers and joining and separating sets

MATERIALS: Cutouts of rocks with numbers 1–12 on them

Guji Guji does not look like the other baby ducks. What does Guji Guji look like? There were other baby ducks, some with stripes and some with spots. Guji Guji tried to count them all and said he counted 12 ducklings. Let's see if we can all count to 12.

Children count to 12.

Guji Guji wants to know if we can help him figure something out. He counted three ducklings with spots and four ducklings with stripes, and he wants to know if there are more ducklings with stripes or spots? How could we find this out? Can you show this with your counters?

Children work on comparing the numbers 3 and 4. The teacher can pose other similar questions with different pairs of numbers.

Guji Guji counts 12 ducks on the bridge. He knows that each duck wants to sit on one of those heavy rocks near the bridge. The rocks are numbered from 1 to 12. I have cutouts of ducks with numbers 1 to 12 on them and cutouts of rocks with numbers 1 to 12 on them. Work with your partner to match each duck's number with the same number on the rock.

Children take time to pair the ducks and rocks. The teacher can have a Velcro version to demonstrate or use an interactive board with 12 ducks and 12 rocks numbered.

In the story, there are crocodiles that show up and have their eyes on the ducks. The crocodiles think the ducks might make good dinner. Guji Guji wants to make sure that the crocodile teeth do not bite his family of ducks. So, Guji Guji calls a dentist to ask if the crocodile teeth could be made less sharp so the ducks could be kept more safe. Of course, the dentist would want to know how many teeth each crocodile has. The dentist would probably also want to know the total number of teeth. Let's see how many teeth we see in the pictures. How could we find out how many teeth each crocodile has and also the total number of teeth the dentist would have to fix? Let's write the numbers on a Post-it note and add to this page in the book so that the next time we read it, we will know exactly how many teeth to worry about.

GEOMETRY: Describing shapes and space

MATERIALS: Pattern blocks, three-dimensional objects, die-cut shapes (optional)

Did you notice in the story that the crocodiles were sharpening their teeth on the trees in the neighborhood? Maybe Guji Guji could think of some way to trick the crocodiles. Maybe he knows that some shapes have very sharp corners, and maybe he could glue the shapes to the trees. Maybe the shapes are made of metal or wood. Do you think that they might hurt a little if a crocodile bit down on a sharp corner? Each time the crocodile would bite the sharp shape on the tree, the corner might hurt the crocodile's mouth a little. Maybe you could help Guji Guji figure out which shapes have sharp corners that he could tie or glue to the trees. Would a circle have a sharp corner? How about a triangle? How about a rectangle? Square? What about a cone? Cylinder?

The teacher can hold up different shapes from pattern blocks, die-cuts, or three-dimensional objects to pose the questions.

MEASUREMENT: Ordering objects by measurable attributes

MATERIALS: String, straws, measuring tape, paper, pencils or crayons

I wonder if Guji Guji ever wondered why he was so much bigger than his other family members. Let's pretend that we happened to be visiting the lake where Guji Guji sat down to think. Maybe he is thinking he wants us to help him find out if he is really a duck or really a crocodile. Do you think we would say something about how tall he was compared with his duckling brothers and sisters? I am holding up some strings, some are as tall as Guji Guji, some are as tall as the ducklings with spots, and the other are as tall as the ducklings with stripes. Which string do you think is as tall as Guji Guji? How do you know?

Children should be able to determine that the longer string is the one that represents Guji Guji.

I'm going to pass these strings out, and I would like you to search for things around the room that are as long as your string. Then we can tell Guji Guji that he and the ducklings are as tall as the objects you find that are the same lengths.

Have the children find objects in the classroom that are the same length as the strings. The teacher can have three strings taped to the board that represent the two ducklings and Guji Guji. Students can tell the teacher what to write next to each string that they find in the room as the same length.

Now, Guji Guji wants to know if he is taller than the distance around your head. This long string is the one we said is as long as Guji Guji. Here is one string for each pair of students. Use the string to determine if Guji Guji is taller than the distance around your head.

Children can compare the length of the string (representing Guji Guji's height) and the distance around their head. Next you can have them see if Guji Guji is taller than the distance from the floor to their belly buttons.

What would we say if Guji Guji said that he did not want to be a big, bad crocodile? We could show him that we are all bigger than ducks too, and we could tell him that we are good people. What if he would want to know how big we are? We could measure ourselves—our height, neck, leg, mouth—right?

The teacher could have tape measures or straws to represent tall blades of grass or thin branches of trees—the perfect size for measuring.

What if Guji Guji lived where there were no big rocks? Do you think we could help Guji Guji find some way to convince the crocodiles to move to some other place to live? Do you think that a wise old owl might come along and remind the crocodiles that the water is deeper and better for hiding in the lake 2 miles away? How far do you think 2 miles is? Guji Guji wants to know how far it is from the school to your home. He wants you to make a map of the route from your home to the school to show him how far it is. Let's work on drawing a map of the route from your home to the school, and let's estimate how far it is. Draw your map and put the estimated number of miles you think it is between your home and school on the bottom.

LESSON PLAN: Kindergarten Example

BOOK: Tierney, F. (2010). *Lion's lunch?* New York: Chicken House. (The cover of *Lion's Lunch?*, by Fiona Tierney and illustrated by Margaret Chamberlain, appears courtesy of Chicken House, an imprint of Scholastic Inc. Copyright © 2010. All rights reserved.)

SYNOPSIS: Sarah walks through the jungle and meets the lion, king of the jungle. The lion threatens to eat Sarah because she was walking through the jungle singing. The lion claims that nobody walks or sings in the jungle. They slither, swoop, gallop, squeak, grunt, chatter, and so forth. When Sarah draws a picture of the lion to show him how mean and mad he is, the lion is angry. He vows to change if Sarah draws a picture of him happy and nice.

NUMBERS AND OPERATIONS: Representing, comparing, and ordering whole numbers and joining and separating sets

MATERIALS: Pictures of some of the animals in the book, tape, large hundreds chart, eight crayons (or straws) for each child or pair of children, two different-colored paper plates for each child or pair of children

Sarah sees all kinds of animals in the jungle. Some of the animals might be friendly to people, and some of the animals might not be so friendly to people. Sarah wants us to make a list of some of the animals she sees and separate them into two groups: friendly and not friendly.

The students can identify some of the animals in the book and decide whether they would be friendly or not. The teacher can have pictures of some of the animals to tape onto the lists along with the word name for the animal. In the story, all the animals except the lion are nice to Sarah, but what if Sarah went into a real jungle? The children may have some debates regarding whether certain animals would be friendly or not. "*Let's count how many animals we have in each group.*" The teacher can help the children count the animals listed in each group and write the number of animals for each group as numerals. Students can practice reading the numerals and count on the hundreds chart until they reach the number of animals in each group.

Sarah is amazed at how well you all can count! She wants us to help her figure out how many animals are in both lists. Do you think we can help her find this out? How could we do this? What are some different ways we could total the number of animals in both groups?

Some ways the children could suggest or the teacher could demonstrate are with base 10 blocks, adding with different manipulatives such as Unifix cubes or chips, adding on with the hundreds chart, and so forth.

Sarah likes to draw pictures of animals. She likes to use crayons to draw pictures just like you like to use crayons to draw pictures. She has a box with eight crayons in it. So to represent the eight crayons, I am going to give each pair of children eight crayons.

The teacher can give each pair of children eight crayons. If crayons are not available, the students can use short straws to represent the crayons. Also, the teacher should give each pair of children two different-colored paper plates.

Let's see how many different ways we can separate the crayons into two groups. For example, we could put two crayons on the red plate and six crayons on the blue plate, or we could put one crayon on the red plate and seven crayons on the blue plate. Take a few minutes to work with your partner to see how many different ways you can find.

Encourage the children to talk about the number of different ways they can divide up eight crayons into two groups.

Very good! I think Sarah will really be pleased to see how many different ways you separated your crayons. Suppose Sarah lost three crayons. Can you talk to your partner and see if you can tell Sarah how many crayons she now has?

Have students explore ways to solve $8 - 3 = 5$.

"Now, let's see how many ways we can separate five crayons into two groups. Use your red and blue plate to find out how many ways there are to separate the five crayons. Be sure to talk to your partners." Teachers can continue with different number of crayons.

 GEOMETRY: Describing shapes and space

MATERIALS: Paper and crayons, plastic bags with different shapes (e.g., large and small triangles, some scalene, right, or obtuse; large and small squares, large and small rectangles) in each for groups of students

"When Sarah draws a picture of the lion being happy, she holds it up so all the animals can see it. What shapes do you see in her drawing?" Children might be able to identify circles and triangles. *"How many circles do you see in her drawing?"* You can have children count the face as one large circle, the two ears, and two eyes. (Some children might want to count the eyeballs as circles). *"How many triangles do you see?"* This may be a little harder to count. Show children how to mark where to start counting, and count the triangles.

So we see Sarah's drawing of a lion that is made of only circles and triangles. I am going to have each of you take a piece of drawing paper and some crayons. I would like you to draw a picture of anything you would like. But your picture should only have circles and triangles in it. Be as creative as you can be, and think about a picture you would like to draw.

After the children draw their pictures, encourage them to talk about their pictures and how many circles and triangles they have drawn in their pictures.

Now the lion wants us to help him. The lion wants Sarah to draw different shapes and tell him stories about the shapes. He wants to learn about the different shapes so he can build some huts in the jungle. The lion wants us to help Sarah draw different shapes and describe the shapes. Sarah made a list of different shapes, and I put the list on the board: circle, square, rectangle, triangle, and semicircle. How could Sarah describe these shapes to the lion? Let's take a few minutes to talk about these shapes.

The teacher can lead the discussion to focus on how many sides, the angles, the characteristics of the shapes, and so forth. *"Now, each group has a plastic bag with different shapes inside. Let's work with our partners to separate the shapes into groups. Decide what your groups will be and be sure each shape is in a group."* As the teacher walks around the groups, pose questions to ask students why they put certain shapes in groups or how they are defining their groups. As a summary, the children can tell Sarah what group they put the different shapes into.

 MEASUREMENT: Ordering objects by measurable attributes

MATERIALS: Cutouts of various animals in the book

Sarah meets all kinds of animals in the jungle. Let's look at a few of the animals. We can see a crocodile, a leopard, and a friendly squirrel on this page on which Sarah is drawing. I have made some cutouts of these animals, and I would like you to think about the size of the ani-

mals. Which animal would you say is the shortest of these three? How do you know this animal is shorter than the other two?

Listen to the description of the measurement terms the child is using. *"Which animal is the tallest of the three? How do you know this animal is taller than the other two? Which animal has the longest tail? How do you know this animal's tail is longer than the other two?"* The dialog can continue with students comparing other animals or other attributes of the animals. It would be helpful to select animals with obvious difference in their measurements. The discussion can focus on the heights or lengths of the animals or their tails.

Suppose the lion asked Sarah to help him draw a fence. He wanted the fence to be tall enough to be sure the animals would not be able to jump over it. Sarah wants us to find out how tall she should draw the fence. Let's think about how tall this fence would need to be. What ideas do you have for Sarah?

The discussion can revolve around the heights of the animals, the ratio of their legs to their body (e.g., the ostrich), how high the animals can jump, or how fast the animals could run to leap over the fence.

First Grade

First-grade Curriculum Focal Points

- **Number and Operations:** Developing understandings of addition and subtraction and strategies for basic addition facts and related subtraction facts

- **Number and Operations:** Developing an understanding of whole number relationships, including grouping of tens and ones

- **Geometry:** Composing and decomposing geometric shapes

 irst-grade mathematics focuses on number relationships and developing the concepts of addition and subtraction. Part–part–whole activities and missing-part activities are common throughout the curriculum. lum. Dot cards and 10 frames are important to help students see numbers in a spatial arrangement and be able to recognize amounts quickly, a process known as *subitizing*. Relationships of *more* and *less* are essential to helping students understand numbers. Number relationships are important to help students develop a "number sense" that enables them to have confidence with quantities and be able to perform mental manipulation (Krasa & Shunkwiler, 2009, p. 25).

LESSON PLAN: First-Grade Example

BOOK: Morrow, B.O. (2009). *Mr. Mosquito put on his tuxedo*. New York: Holiday House. (Book cover illustration copyright ©2009 by Ponder Goembel from *Mr. Mosquito Put on His Tuxedo* by Barbara Olenyik Morrow. All rights reserved. Reprinted by permission of Holiday House, Inc.)

SYNOPSIS: Insects decide to hold a dance ball in a tent while a family sleeps. A big bear stomps close to the tent and the mosquitoes are called upon to attack the bear. Mr. Mosquito, who is dressed in a tuxedo, leads his brigade of mosquitoes to get rid of the bear and save the other insects. The Queen Bee honors Mr. Mosquito for his outstanding

82   Wilburne, Keat, and Napoli

leadership. The story of Mr. Mosquito to the rescue features hilarious text and witty, vivid illustrations.

NUMBER AND OPERATIONS AND ALGEBRA: Developing understandings of addition
and subtraction and strategies for basic
addition facts and related subtraction
facts

MATERIALS: Counters or Unifix cubes (optional)

*I just heard that Mr. Mosquito needs more mosquitoes to help get rid of the big bear in the
story. He needs a back-up team. Let's pretend we are all mosquitoes. What can you tell us about
mosquitoes? Let's dance around the room like mosquitoes without touching each other.*

Children should buzz and pretend to have a stinger.

*The lightning bugs also want to help get rid of the bear by flashing their bright lights in the
bear's face. Mr. Mosquito calls for 10 insects to attack the bear, and the insects need to be mosquitoes and lightning bugs. How many mosquitoes and how many lightning bugs are needed
to attack the bear?*

Children can look for two addends whose sum is 10. Sample solutions include two lightning
bugs and eight mosquitoes, three lightning bugs and seven mosquitoes, and so forth.

*In the story the Queen Bee wants to have a parade to celebrate the fact that they were able to
get rid of the bear. She asked Mr. Mosquito to organize the insects into rows to march around
the tent. She wants each row to have a different pattern with the insects. What patterns of insects can you help Mr. Mosquito create?*

For example, a pattern could be bed bug, horsefly, bed bug, horsefly, and so forth. The
teacher could also have students pretend they were different insects and arrange themselves in patterns.

*Let's pretend we are all insects and we are marching in rows. How can we arrange ourselves to
march in rows? How could we figure this out? You have counters on your tables and paper and
pencil to help you find a solution.*

Answers will vary depending on the number of children.

NUMBER AND OPERATIONS: Developing an understanding of whole number relationships, including grouping in tens and ones

MATERIALS: Sock, granola bar, licorice string, or other nonstandard units; base 10 blocks

*Because Mr. Mosquito is now the Royal Pest, the Queen Bee gives him a map. He sent us this
map so we can help him solve a problem. The map shows us where there are beehives for the
bees to make honey. The beehives are in danger because they are so close to the bear's cave.
The bees want the ants to help them move the beehives because the ants can carry a lot of
weight.*

Point out to the children how the ants are carrying Mr. Mosquito on the cover of the book.

*The ants want us to find the shortest route to bring the beehives closer to the lookout house.
Let's pretend in our classroom that the door is where the lookout station is located, and the
light switch, thermostat, and the easel are where the beehives are located. Let's measure the
distance using some of the items from the tent in the story, such as a sock, granola bar, licorice
string, and so forth.*

Students can work in small groups to measure the distance between items with the different nonstandard units. Some discussion regarding how to measure the distance might be needed. The teacher can have the students put their measurements on a chart at the front of the room.

Well done! I'm sure the ants would be very proud of how well you worked to find the measurements. But what if Mr. Mosquito does not understand what these numbers mean? Can you change your measurements into groups of tens and ones to show him what each measurement represents? He also wants us to show him with base 10 blocks what the distance to each beehive would be so he can tell the ants. So, let's show the distance to each beehive with the base 10 blocks at your tables.

GEOMETRY: Composing and decomposing geometric shapes

MATERIALS: Cutout shapes of triangles, squares, rectangles, and circles (approximately four per child)

The insects decide to build a lookout house (or fort) to keep an eye out for any more bears or other scary animals that might want to eat them. What kinds of things could they use to make a lookout house?

The students should be encouraged to think of ideas.

We need to build some possible lookout houses for Mr. Mosquito. Mr. Mosquito wants us to make lookout houses using four squares, four triangles, four rectangles, and four circles. Let's use our cutout pieces of squares, triangles, rectangles, and circles to see what kind of lookout houses we could make to show Mr. Mosquito.

Students should use the cutout shapes or blocks to create possible lookout houses. The teacher should have the students describe their lookout houses to Mr. Mosquito, being sure to use their mathematical vocabulary and position words such as *above, next to, below,* and so forth.

Now, the Queen Bee wants us to help her again. She wants us to tell her what is the same and what is different about some of the insects. She suggested that we create a Venn diagram to show her how some pairs of insects are the same and how they are different. For example, let's look at the ladybugs and the ants. What is the same about them and what is different?

The teacher can draw a large Venn diagram and fill it in based on responses from the students; other possible comparisons with other sets of insects can be made. Classification activities and Venn diagrams help students use problem-solving skills and logical reasoning. This activity also connects science to mathematics.

Very good, children! The Queen Bee has decided to have another fancy ball, but this time, she only wants the insects that have lines of symmetry to be invited. She wants us to look at the pictures of the insects in the book and see which insects she should invite. Can we help her find the insects to be invited?

Understanding symmetry is important to help students examine shapes and determine how many lines of symmetry they have. The lines of symmetry can lead to discussions about rotational symmetry in later grades.

LESSON PLAN: First-Grade Example

BOOK: Bryan, A. (2003). *Beautiful blackbird*. New York: Atheneum Books for Young Readers.

Beautiful Blackbird

SYNOPSIS: Ashley Bryan uses gorgeous and colorful collage images in this adaptation of an African folk tale from the Ila-speaking people of Zambia. Blackbird shares his gifts with the other birds and gives a little bit of his blackening brew to all of the birds but reminds them that real beauty comes from the inside.

NUMBER AND OPERATIONS: Developing understandings of addition and subtraction and strategies for basic addition facts and related subtraction facts

MATERIALS: Stickers, copies of the pages, Unifix cubes, chart paper, colored pencils (all optional)

The teacher can begin the lesson by saying, *"What a wonderful story with a beautiful message. Do you know that our class received some mail today? Yes, we received a letter from Beautiful Blackbird. Let's read it together."* The teacher can write a letter from Beautiful Blackbird with problem posing prompts.

Dear First-Grade Friends,

Hi! Hope that you enjoyed my story! I really need your help. There are so many birds in my village that I can't figure out how many invitations to write for my birthday party. Do you think that you can help me? I don't know where to start! Thank you so much for your help.

Coo-coo-roo, Coo-ca-roo!
Beautiful Blackbird

Well, it looks like Beautiful Blackbird needs our help. Do you think that we can help him? I bet we can. What are your ideas? How can we help him figure out how many birds there are in the village? Let's take a careful look at the first two pages. There are indeed many birds in the village. How should we count them?

The children should be encouraged to brainstorm some possible ways to count all the birds on pages 1 and 2 of the book. Some possible ways might be to touch the birds and count them, place a sticker on the birds as they are counted, copy the pages and cut the birds out to count them, count them by color, and so forth.

The teacher continues, *"Well, there are many different colors of birds, aren't there? What if we decided to make a graph to show Blackbird how many different-colored birds there are? How could we make a graph?"* The students should be encouraged to see how many different ways they could make a graph.

With the class, the teacher can work with the students to count the different number of birds and create a graph that will be used for additional problem-solving experiences.

Note: There are other ways to sort the birds: by size, by the number of feathers, by the birds with headdresses and birds without headdresses, by the color of the birds' eyes (e.g., some have blue, some have pink), and so forth.

NUMBER AND OPERATIONS: Developing an understanding of whole number relationships, including grouping of tens and ones

MATERIALS: Unifix cubes, counters, or base 10 pieces, hundreds chart (optional)

Color	Number of Blackbird's friends
Yellow or golden	6
Blue	5
Magenta or purple	3
Red	6
Green	5
Orange	9
Gray	7
Pink	4
Tan	4

Wow! Blackbird has a lot of friends. Now he has another problem. He wants to have his party at the Village Park, but the park ranger only allows 10 birds in each tree. Why do you think they only allow 10 birds in each tree?

Dear First-Grade Friends,

Thank you so very much for helping me to find out how many birds are in my village. Now, I can send them invitations to my birthday party. You were so helpful that I hope you can help me out again! Here is what I need help with:

I need to order some cupcakes for my party. It's a funny thing in my village. The birds like to eat the same color cupcake as their feathers. So, what kind of cake will the yellow birds like to eat? (Lemon is one possible answer.) Blue birds? (Blueberry is one possible answer.) So how many types of each cupcake should I order?

I also want to make some goodie bags for my friends. I want to put 10 pieces of candy in each bag, and I have bubble gum pieces and gummy worms. How many different ways can I put the bubble gum pieces and gummy worms in each bag to have 10 pieces (e.g., 1 piece of bubble gum and 9 gummy worms)?

I also know some of my friends like lollipops. If I decide to add lollipops to the goodie bags and still have 10 pieces of candy in each bag, how many different ways can we make goodie bags?

Sincerely,
Beautiful Blackbird

The students should be encouraged to come up with their own ideas. "*How can we help Blackbird figure out how many trees he will need to reserve? Maybe we could show him with our Unifix cubes* (or flannel board pieces)." The teacher should have the students brainstorm and then use Unifix cubes to represent the birds by grouping by tens and ones.

"*Boys and girls, we received another letter from our friend, Blackbird. Let's read what he has to say.*"

The teacher continues, "*Let's see if we can help Blackbird solve these problems.*" The students should use their problem-solving strategies to solve, such as guess and check, make a table, draw pictures, and so forth.

"*Oh no! I just received an e-mail from Ringdove, one of Blackbird's friends. There is trouble in the village. We need to help him out.*"

We have been such great first-grade helpers. I think that we can help Ringdove and the birds in the village again, don't you? Let's use our counters to represent the birds with headdresses.

To: First-Grade Class (e-mail)
From: ringdove@village.com
Re: Help needed fast!
Date: 9/9/11

Oh, coo-coo-roo, Coo-ca-roo! Friends, Black-bird just asked me if I would order the party hats and crowns for the birds to wear. I need to know how many birds there are with headdresses so I know how many crowns to order. Also, I need to know how many birds do not have headdresses so I know how many party hats to order. Can you help me figure this out? Please, please help me!

Love,
Your friend Ringdove

Guess what, class! We just received an invitation to Blackbird's party to meet Blackbird and his friends. How many cupcakes would he need to order now? Wait a minute—we know that some of us like vanilla cupcakes and others like chocolate cupcakes. How could we find out how many different flavors of cupcakes he should order?

Students might suggest taking a poll by having students in the class raise their hand if they want vanilla.

I just heard that Blackbird wants everyone to have an ice cream cone along with the cupcakes. He wants to know how many scoops of ice cream to order if each of us has two scoops of ice cream on a cone. Can you help him figure this out? What if he wanted each of us to have three scoops of ice cream on a cone? How many scoops of ice cream would he need to order?

The teacher can encourage students to act this out with Unifix cubes or use their hundreds board to count by twos and threes.

MEASUREMENT: Measuring with nonstandard unit of measurement

MATERIALS: Construction paper cutouts of birds or feathers, crepe paper

Little Blackbird wants us to bring some crepe paper decorations for the trees. He wanted to have some crepe paper strings that are the same length as the wingspans of the birds. He thought we could pretend we were birds and measure our wingspans with crepe paper. He then wants us to put the strings of crepe paper in order from the shortest piece to the longest piece. He loves our classroom and needs our help to be sure that it is just right! Do you want to help him with this important job?

Students can work in pairs to measure their wingspans with crepe paper and put a piece of tape on the end to post it to the board. They should be encouraged to post them in order from smallest wingspan to largest. The teacher might want to encourage the children to discuss why there are different sizes of wingspans.

I like how we all measured our wingspans. What if Blackbird wanted us to measure the length of some items in our classroom? He wants to know how many feathers long the item is and how many bird lengths the item is. Let's see if we can show Blackbird how long the items are in our classroom.

The teacher might want to make a chart and select certain items in the classroom that the children can measure with a feather or cutout of a bird. The chart can include as many items as the children want to measure, time permitting.

Classroom item	How many feathers is it?	How many birds is it?
Blackboard		
Student desk		
Teacher desk		
Pencil box		
Closet		
Reading book		
Window sill		
Book shelf		

GEOMETRY: Composing and decomposing geometric shapes

MATERIALS: Pattern blocks

First-grade friends, do you remember when Blackbird asked us for our help in measuring differ-ent items in our class? Well, he also invited us to make special designs for the village school. Would you like to help them out? What if we take our pattern blocks to make new designs? Let's try to use our pattern blocks to make a new shape that has four sides.

The teacher can have the students compare their shapes and talk about the properties of their shapes. *"Now, let's use our pattern blocks to make a new shape that has five sides. Can you make a shape with two tiles that has a line of symmetry?"* A sample answer is shown below.

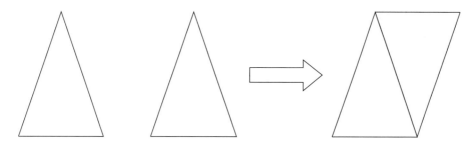

Second Grade

econd-grade mathematics emphasizes helping students learn strategies to become proficient in their basic addition and subtraction facts and become fluent using these facts. They need to practice their facts and begin to use the facts to do two- and three-digit addition and subtraction problems. They should understand the inverse relationship between addition and subtraction and the properties of commutativity and associativity. They need experience with composing and decomposing numbers, estimating, and rounding numbers. Place value and the base 10 numeration system are important concepts to help students understand regrouping or trading in multidigit addition and subtraction. Also, measurement is a topic of considerable importance. Students need experience with the process of measurement and understanding what the unit value represents. They should be able to understand the concept of transitivity (i.e., if A is longer than B, and if B is longer than C, then A is longer than C).

Using storybooks can help teachers create authentic problems to engage students in computation strategies, place value, and measuring activities. For example, one teacher had the students pretend they were at the restaurant, and they were going to eat some of the food carried by the waitress in the story *Minnie's Diner: A Multiplying Menu* (Dodds, 2004). She had a list of the food on a chart at the front of the classroom, and students used their base 10 blocks to determine how much their meals would cost them. Then they recorded their problems and drew pictures to represent the food they were ordering. In another classroom, a teacher had students use square tiles to determine how many customers could sit along the perimeter of the table if each side could fit one person. She then gave them two, three, and four squares and asked them to explore the number of customers who could be seated if the tables were placed side by side. Next, she had them create a chart with the information to look for patterns between the number of square tables and the number of customers that could be seated. This activity branched into algebraic thinking without any mention of algebra in the story.

Let's look at two storybooks and the mathematics problems that teachers posed for each focal point.

LESSON PLAN: Second-Grade Example

BOOK: Plourde, L. (2007). *A mountain of mittens*. Watertown, MA: Charlesbridge (Cover art reproduced by permission by Charlesbridge Publishing, Inc.)

SYNOPSIS: Every morning Molly's parents remind her to come home after school with her mittens, and every day Molly forgets. Nothing works—not Velcro, not yarn, not crochet chains, not even duct tape. But Molly is not alone. All the kids at school forget, and soon there is a mountain of mittens in lost-and-found that has grown out of control.

NUMBER AND OPERATIONS: Developing an understanding of the base 10 numeration system and place-value concepts

MATERIALS: Base 10 blocks

The teacher begins the lesson as follows:

Oh my! The principal in the story, Mrs. Folly, said that no one could leave school until they reclaimed their mittens. The book shows a picture of a huge pile of mittens. How many mittens do you think could be in that pile? Let's go around the room and have everyone give us an estimate number of mittens.

The teacher solicits responses and writes them on the board.

Wow, there are many different estimates for the number of mittens. What is the largest estimate? Can you show Mrs. Folly how to make that number with your base 10 blocks? What is the smallest estimate? Let's show Mrs. Folly how to make that number with our base 10 blocks. What if Mrs. Folly counted all the mittens and there were 124 mittens in the pile; can you show her how to represent 124 with base 10 blocks? How could we represent 124 if we did not have any hundreds blocks?

The teacher solicits responses such as 12 (tens) and 4 (ones) or 10 (tens) and 24 (ones). "*How many different ways could we represent 124 with our blocks?*" The teacher could make a list of the different ways and encourage students to look for a pattern.

What if our principal wanted to know how many mittens would be piled high in the gym if everyone in our school left their mittens? How many mittens do you think there might be? How could we figure this out?

Various strategies are possible. "*What if everyone in our class left their mittens at school, how many mittens would that be? Talk to your partners and determine how many mittens would be left. Each mitten is counted individually.*" Students work with partners to find a solution and present their process and solution to the class. "*What if every student in our class left their mittens every day of this week, how many mittens would be in a pile?"* The teacher continues the lesson as follows:

Molly found 15 mittens in the large pile at her school, but she knows she lost 24 mittens because she lost one pair every day for 12 days. How many more mittens does she need to find? What is the greatest amount of mittens she could have lost in a month? What is the greatest amount of mittens she could have lost in 3 months? Take a few minutes with your partners and try to help Molly find solutions to these problems.

MEASUREMENT: Developing an understanding of linear measurement and facility with measuring lengths

MATERIALS: Paper, crayons, scissors

Molly had several pairs of mittens in the story. She wants to know what our mittens would look like if we were to make a pair. Let's make our own pair of mittens. On your tables, you have some paper and crayons. Hold up one of your hands to show me what a mitten would cover. Very good! Now trace your hand on the paper so you can make a paper pair of mittens. It should have room for a thumb and four fingers. After you trace your hand, use the scissors carefully to cut out your mittens. Then put your name on your paper mittens.

The students then take some time to cut out their mittens.

Wow, look at all the paper mittens we have in our classroom! Remember in the story how Molly put a mitten on the classroom turtle to keep him warm? How did she know the turtle would fit inside her mitten?

The students can offer various responses.

Molly wants to know what is inside our classroom that could fit into your mittens. She would like us to make a list of the things in our classroom that fit into our mittens. Use your mittens as a measuring tool to find two things in the classroom that could fit into your mitten and put the items on your desk.

The students walk around the room to find two objects. Some discussion can occur regarding how they know the item would fit inside their mitten. The teacher can make a list of the items on the board.

Now, Mrs. Folly wants us to measure the length of our desks with our mittens. How could we use our mittens to measure the length of the desks? Work with your partners to determine how long your desk is in mitten length.

The teacher should walk around the room to observe the process students are using to measure the length. Some students may not understand the iterative process needed to find the length and will need the teacher to scaffold their learning through questions. The teacher can compare the lengths of the desks and question students regarding why there are different measurements when the desks are the same size.

LESSON PLAN: Second-Grade Example

BOOK: Chamberlin, M., & Chamberlin, R. (2005). *Mama Panya's pancakes: A village tale from Kenya.* Cambridge, MA: Barefoot Books. (Cover art reproduced by permission.)

SYNOPSIS: On market day, Mama Panya's son, Adika, invites everyone he sees to a pancake dinner. How will Mama Panya ever feed them all? This clever and heartwarming story about Kenyan village life teaches the importance of sharing, even when you have little to give.

NUMBER AND OPERATIONS: Developing quick recall of addition facts and related sub-
                               traction facts and fluency with multidigit addition and
                               subtraction

MATERIALS: Counters, hundreds chart

The teacher begins with several questions such as *"How many of you like pancakes?"* *"What do you like on your pancakes?"* *"How many pancakes can you eat?"* *"Let's count how many people Adika invites to his mama's for pancakes."* As the teacher counts the number of people with the students in the class, they should see that seven people were invited. There is a dog on every page who follows Adika, so the class could discuss whether to count the dog as someone who will eat some pancakes.

So, if we count Adika and his mama and the seven people who were invited, how many people will be at the pancake dinner? Adika's mama wants us to help her find out how many pancakes she needs to make. She is not sure how many pancakes each person will eat. Do you think we can help her out? Let's use our counters and hundreds chart to figure out how many pancakes mama will need to make if everyone eats two pancakes. Then we will find out how many pancakes she will need to make if everyone eats three pancakes, four pancakes, and five pancakes. Do you think the people in the story will be able to eat six pancakes each?

Students can use their counters to determine the number of pancakes for each question. *"Let's write some number sentences to go along with the number of pancakes for each person. If everyone eats two pancakes, what would our number sentence be?"* The students should respond with 9 + 9 = 18. The teacher continues, *"Very good. Let's write a number sentence that would show how to represent the number of pancakes if everyone ate three pancakes."* The students need to correctly respond with 9 + 9 + 9 = 27. Continue with the number sentences for four and five pancakes.

NUMBERS AND OPERATIONS: Developing an understanding of the base 10 numeration
                                system and place-value concepts

MATERIALS: Base 10 blocks (optional)

Adika loves to skip in the book, doesn't he? He is always a few steps ahead of his mama. Let's say it takes him 14 skips to get from one tent to another tent and 36 skips to get from the tent to the market. Adika wants us to help him figure out how many skips he took altogether. Use your base 10 blocks if you need to, and use your whiteboards to write the number sentence.

The students work on the two-digit addition problem. *"Now, Adika counted his skips and did 245 skips on Saturday. That is a lot of skips, isn't it? He wants us to show him what 245 looks like with our base 10 blocks."* Students represent the number 245 with the blocks.

Well done; I see everyone has 245 represented with the blocks. Can someone tell Adika how many hundreds are in 245? How many tens are in 245? How many ones are in 245? On Sunday, Adika skipped 248 skips total. Did he skip more on Saturday or on Sunday? How can we convince Adika which day he had more skips?

Students can show with blocks or by explaining that there are more ones in 248 with the same number of hundreds and tens. The teacher can select any three-digit numbers to have students compare and order the numbers.

Adika sees lots of animals along the way to the market. Some monkeys and tigers are illustrated on the pages. As he was skipping, he thought about a number puzzle, and he wanted to see if we could help him solve it.

MEASUREMENT: Developing an understanding of linear measurement and facility in measuring lengths

MATERIALS: Rulers, string (optional)

The teacher begins the lesson by saying, *"Do you see the butterfly in the story? In Kenya, they have butterflies that have the largest wingspan."* (This is according to the information in the back of the book.)

Who can tell us what a wingspan is? Can you show us what we mean by wingspan? The people in Kenya have measured the wingspan of this butterfly, and it measures 9 inches. I wonder how long 9 inches is? Let's have you each come to the board and draw a line that you think measures 9 inches long. Be sure to put your initials next to your line so you will know which line is yours.

Dear Boys and Girls in Second Grade,

I saw 38 animals on my way to the market: some monkeys and some tigers. I saw more monkeys than tigers. There were an even number of tigers, so would there be an even or an odd number of monkeys? Take a minute to discuss this and see if you can convince your classmates whether there was an even or an odd number of monkeys. (There has to be an even number of monkeys because an EVEN + EVEN = EVEN, and we know the number of tigers is even and the total number of animals was even.)

After you figure this out, try to find the number of monkeys I saw. The number of tigers I saw had a tens digit that was odd and a ones digit that was more than 6. Can you find out how many tigers I saw? Use the clues I gave you. (There must be 18 tigers. A tens digit that was odd tells us that it must be one. A three in the tens place would be too much if there were only 38 animals and there were more monkeys than tigers. The ones digit is more than 6, and we know there is an even number of tigers. So, that would mean the ones digit must be an 8.) Now, can you figure out how many monkeys I saw? (There were 38 animals and 18 tigers, so there must be 38 – 18 = 20 monkeys.) Thank you for helping me with this number puzzle.

Sincerely,
Adika

Students come to the board and draw a line they believe would be 9 inches long. This could also be done by having students cut a piece of string where they believe it measures 9 inches or tear toilet paper off a roll where they believe it measures 9 inches. *"Wow, there are many different lines and lengths. Each of you has a ruler, so I would like you to put your finger on the 9-inch mark."* The teacher can walk around and check to be sure students have their finger on the 9-inch mark.

Now that you each know where the 9-inch mark is, I would like you to come up to the line that you drew and measure it. I would also like you to mark off where the 9-inch mark would be on your line. Let me show you what I mean.

The teacher models how students can measure their line and write the length of their line next to it. Then, mark off where 9 inches would be on their line.

How many of you drew a line that was longer than 9 inches? How many of you drew a line that was shorter than 9 inches? Did anyone draw a line that measured exactly 9 inches? I know we are all good at measuring. Now, imagine a beautiful butterfly flying around our classroom that has a wingspan of 9 inches!

Third Grade

Third-grade Curriculum Focal Points

- **Number and Operations and Algebra:** Developing understandings of multiplication and division and strategies for basic multiplication facts and related division facts

- **Number and Operations:** Developing an understanding of fractions and fraction equivalence

- **Geometry:** Describing and analyzing properties of two-dimensional shapes

he third-grade curriculum focuses on helping students understand the meaning of multiplication and division of whole numbers through the use of representations (e.g., equal-sized groups, arrays, area models, equal "jumps" on number lines for multiplication, and successive subtraction, partitioning, and sharing for division). They use properties of addition and multiplication (e.g., commutativity, associativity, distributive property) to multiply whole numbers and apply increasingly sophisticated strategies based on these properties to solve multiplication and division problems involving basic facts. By comparing a variety of solution strategies, students relate multiplication and division as inverse operations.

Beginning work with fractions is another essential concept in third grade. The curriculum should focus on tasks that help students understand the meaning of fractions and develop "fraction sense." They should be able to represent fractional parts with area models such as grids, pizzas, or candy bars. Students may be able to represent fractional parts with set models by using concrete materials such as colored counters or Unifix cubes, and they should be able to represent fractions on a number line. They might be able to think about fractions as numbers and explore relationships between fractions, such as knowing which fractions are equivalent, finding fractions between fractions, and estimating whether a fraction is closer to 0 or 1. Because fractions are often a difficult area for many students, early hands-on explorations with manipulatives to compare fractional pieces and see the relationship between fractional numbers are critical. Story-books with fractional concepts are not that common, so teachers need to be cre-ative and willing to find situations in a story in which they can have students think about fractions. For example, *The Patchwork Quilt* (Flournoy, 1985) is a story about a grandmother who makes a special quilt for a girl named Tanya. One third-grade teacher shared how she has her students discuss the fractional part of dif-ferent pieces of a fabric on the quilt in the storybook pictures and extends the dis-cussions to pose a problem asking students to make a square with one half of it covered with a fabric. How could Tanya use the fabric to cover one half of the quilt? This teacher encouraged her students to use a geoboard to show the differ-ent ways to divide a square into one half. She also had her students compare dif-ferent squares of the quilt to see which had the larger fractional part covered. Her lesson extended to representing mixed numbers with the quilt squares.

LESSON PLAN: Third-Grade Example

BOOK: Feiffer, J. (1999). *Meanwhile*. New York: HarperCollins Publishing. (Book Cover illustration copyright © 1999 by Jules Feiffer from Meanwhile. All rights reserved. Reprinted by permission of Harper Collins, Inc.)

SYNOPSIS: Raymond is tired of his mother interrupting his quiet time to have him do household chores. He wishes he could just change his situation like how it happens in storybooks. He writes the word *meanwhile* to change his situation and confronts different fantasy lands to escape doing his chores. The first fantasy land he enters is on a pirate ship.

NUMBER AND OPERATIONS AND ALGEBRA: Developing understandings of multi-plication and division and strategies for basic multiplication facts and related division facts

MATERIALS: Counters

The first story in this book provides many different mathematical problems Raymond or other characters could face on the ship and problems that could be created with a pirate setting. The teacher might begin the lesson plan as follows:

We see how the pirates are forcing Raymond to walk the plank, and he does not want to walk the plank. He does not want to be forced to jump off the plank and be fed to the sharks that might be in the ocean. So Raymond has a plan. He decides to try to barter with the pirates. Can anyone explain what it means to barter with someone?

The teacher solicits responses from the students.

Well, all of a sudden, Raymond remembers that he has some baseball cards in his pocket and he decides to try and trade his 24 baseball cards for his freedom. The pirates grumble as they try to figure out how many baseball cards each pirate would get if they divided the cards up equally. Let's think about how many baseball cards each pirate would get if there were four pi-

rates. Pretend the counters on your tables are baseball cards. Count out 24 counters and work in your pairs to determine how to divide them up into four piles to represent the four pirates.

After the students solve this problem, the teacher could ask them to determine how many baseball cards each pirate would get if there were 6, 8, or 12 pirates.

The students can use counters to represent the baseball cards, and the teacher can show them how they would divide them up evenly so that each pirate would have an equal amount.

"Let's think about another problem. What if there were 10 pirates? How could Raymond divide up the 24 baseball cards among 10 pirates?" A discussion can follow regarding how to handle the remainders when 24 is divided by 10.

What do you think would happen if one of the pirates decides he does not want baseball cards, and he convinces the other pirates that they do not need baseball cards? Raymond begins to panic. What could he think of next? He thinks and thinks. What else do you think Raymond could have in his pocket that he could use to barter with?

The students are encouraged to brainstorm what other items Raymond could have in his pocket (e.g., candy bars, pens, markers, small toys, shiny coins). The teacher then poses problems similar to the preceding one: What if there were six pirates and Raymond had 20 silver coins? How could he divide up the number of coins so that each pirate would get an equal amount? Or what if there were eight pirates and Raymond had 30 crayons in his pocket?

In the second fantasy land, Raymond visits the Wild West. *"Raymond was attacked by a posse of six law-abiding officials because they thought he was a bandit. Why do you think they thought he was a bandit?"* Wait for responses from the students.

When Raymond takes his mask off to show them he is an ordinary citizen, the posse is shocked to see he is not a bandit. Then Raymond tells the posse that he has not had a thing to eat since yesterday. The posse of six officials each gave Raymond the same number of cookies. Raymond counts and sees he has 30 cookies. Can you figure out how many cookies each official gave him? Can someone tell us what the number sentence is that we need to figure out?

Students should see that the number sentence would be $30 \div 6 = x$. *"Good work. Now let's use our counters again to see if we can help Raymond figure this out."* The teacher should encourage the students to share their strategies for how they determined the number of cookies each official gave to Raymond. To have students extend their knowledge of division and think about a problem that has multiple answers, one possibility is as follows:

Great work. Now let's think about this a little differently. What if there were four officials who had cookies in their backpacks, and they each gave Raymond either three or four cookies? How many cookies total could Raymond have? What strategies might help us solve this problem?

The students should be given time to work on the problem without guidance or hints at first. If they appear to be struggling, the teacher might suggest that there are four officials, each giving Raymond either three cookies or four cookies. The teacher then asks the students what strategies might be helpful to organize this information and the total number of cookies. If they consider making a chart, they could label the top of each column as #1, #2, #3, and #4, representing the four officials. Each row could represent the number of cookies each official gave to Raymond. Raymond would receive either 12, 13, 14, 15, or 16 cookies. A sample chart follows:

Official #1	Official #2	Official #3	Official #4	Total cookies
3	3	3	3	12
3	3	3	4	13
3	3	4	4	14
3	4	4	4	15
4	3	3	3	13
4	4	3	3	14
4	4	4	3	15
4	4	4	4	16

Some problems that might be posed around Raymond and the Wild West are as follows:

As Raymond tries to leave the Wild West, a mountain lion threatens to pounce on him. Raymond is frightened but remembers the cookies he has in his pocket. He decides to drop one cookie every three steps in hopes that the mountain lion would focus on eating the cookies instead of eating him. Can we help Raymond determine how many steps he would need to take until all 30 cookies are gone? Again, let's use our counters to represent the 30 cookies and work in our small groups to help Raymond find the answer.

In the third story, Raymond visits space and talks to martians.

How amazing that Raymond now believes he is in space and seeing martians. He sees that there are 32 martian spaceships. If there are some two-headed and some one-headed martians in the ships, how many of each could there be in the 32 spaceships? What are some ways that Raymond could figure this out? Let's make some lists to see the possible solutions to this problem.
    As Raymond flies around, he sees there are 30 martian spaceships docked at the space station. He sees that some of the ships have three antennas and some of the ships have four antennas. How many three-antenna ships and how many four-antenna ships could there be if there are thirty of them docked at the station? Talk about ways you might be able to figure this out with your partners.

With both martian spaceship problems, the goal is to have students use various problem-solving strategies to solve them. Some students might draw pictures of one-headed and two-headed martians or three-antenna and four-antenna spaceships, other students might create a table, and others might use guess and check. The teacher should have students share their strategies with the class and encourage them to model their thinking in front of the other students. The teacher should also emphasize that there is no one right way to solve this problem and how the students solved the problem is what is most important.

NUMBER AND OPERATIONS: Developing an understanding of fractions and fraction equivalence

MATERIALS: Large newsprint (optional)

In the pirate story, Raymond is forced to walk the plank.

Raymond is surprised to see that the pirates have marks on the plank. They marked off ¼, ½, and ¾ of the way to the edge of the plank. Raymond says the plank is 12 feet long. He wants us

to find the distance on the plank that would be ½, ¼, and ¾. Work with your partner to find the distance on the plank that would be ¼, ½, and ¾ of the plank.

The teacher walks around the classroom, noticing the various strategies students use to solve this problem. The teacher then has pairs of students explain their solution to the class. The teacher could also cut a large sheet of newsprint paper to represent the plank and have students determine where the ¼, ½, and ¾ point would be on the paper plank. The teacher asks them how they could figure this out if they did not have a ruler.

Now, Raymond has another problem. He likes to count with fractions. He wants to know if we can count from 0 to 4 by fourths. Let's look at a number line on the board that is marked off from 0 to 4. We need some volunteers to help us mark off the ¼, ½, and ¾ parts of each whole.

The teacher selects various students to mark off the fractional values. "*Great, this will help us count by fourths. Let's all count together: 0, ¼, ½, ¾, 1, 1¼, 1½, 1¾, 2, . . .*" The teacher has the students count by fourths with and without looking at the number line. The teacher poses additional questions, such as "*Can we count by halves to 4?*" "*What if Raymond wanted us to count by fourths to 6? Can we try this?*"

Raymond likes to write fractions and stories with fractions. He wants us to find some fractions that have a value less than 1 with a numerator that is even and a denominator that is odd and less than 10. How many fractions can we write that satisfy his rule? Are any of those fractions equivalent to each other?

GEOMETRY: Describing and analyzing properties of two-dimensional shapes

MATERIALS: Colored pencils or crayons (optional)

In the pirate scene, the beautiful maiden tries to save Raymond by offering the pirates some of her jewels.

In the book, the beautiful maiden shows the pirates a blue sapphire jewel and tells them it is a special jewel because it is in the shape of a parallelogram. The captain of the pirates asks her how she knows it is a parallelogram. She describes the properties of her jewel and convinces the captain that it is truly a parallelogram. What properties could she have told the captain?

Some responses could include that a parallelogram has opposite sides congruent and parallel, opposite angles are congruent, the shape is a quadrilateral, and so forth. Discussions can continue by selecting different two-dimensional shapes for jewels and having the students describe the shapes. Students can be encouraged to draw a picture of a treasure chest full of jewels of different shapes or a chest half full of jewels of different shapes.

Further extensions of this book include focusing on the communication and connection process standards and encouraging students to write their own *Meanwhile* scenario or write their own story problems.

LESSON PLAN: Third-Grade Example

BOOK: Grandits, J. (2009). *The travel game.* New York: Clarion Books. (Cover art reproduced by permission.)

SYNOPSIS: Tad helps his family work in their tailor shop in Buffalo, New York. He also loves to play the travel game with his Aunt Hattie. To play the travel game, you spin a globe, close your eyes, and put your finger down—and that's where you will go! The pictures in the almanac set the scenes; your imagination takes care of the rest.

NUMBER AND OPERATIONS AND ALGEBRA: Developing understandings of multiplication and division and strategies for basic multiplication facts and related division facts

MATERIALS: Counters or Unifix cubes (optional)

Let's say you are tailors working in the Tailor Shop with Tad and his family. You are in charge of ordering all the buttons of different colors and shapes for the pants, coats, and so forth. If Uncle Myron makes suits and needs to put six brown round buttons on each suit coat, how many coats could he make if you ordered two dozen brown round buttons? Take a minute in your groups and use your counters to help you figure this out.

The teacher encourages the students to share their strategies.

Let's look at another situation in the tailor shop. If suit coats for the extra tall men take nine brown round buttons, how many suit coats can you make with the two dozen brown buttons you ordered? What if each suit coat for the extra wide men take eight black square buttons? How many suit coats could you make with three dozen black square buttons?

Students continue to work in groups and use counters to find the solutions. The teacher has several students share their strategies with the class.

   "*What if there were two dozen tan buttons? The green ladies' jackets take four tan buttons and the blue ladies' jackets take three tan buttons. How many jackets can be made?*" The teacher encourages students to use various strategies to solve the problem and to look for more than one solution. The students should find that the tailor could make six green ladies' jackets, eight blue ladies' jackets, or three green jackets and four blue jackets.

Now the tailor wants to know if it takes more tan buttons to make four blue jackets and three green jackets, or three blue jackets and four green jackets, or would the jackets require the same amount of buttons? Work with your partner to see if you can help the tailor solve this problem. Be sure you can you prove your answer.

The students could draw pictures, make a table, or model the problem with counters to determine that the four blue jackets and three green jackets require 24 tan buttons and the three blue jackets and four green jackets require 25 tan buttons.

   In the story, Tad visits the boat city in Hong Kong.

Can you imagine living on a boat all the time? The boat city even has water taxis to help people get from one place to another, just like there are taxis in our city (town). Tad sees that there is one boat in the boat city that has 24 people living on it. Let's suppose all 24 people wanted to take a water taxi to go into town to shop. But the green water taxis can only carry four people (not counting the taxi driver), and the blue water taxis can only carry five people (not counting the taxi driver). How many ways could the people load the water taxis to get to town? Let's work in our small groups and see how many different ways the 24 people could load onto the taxis to head to shore. There is one rule that the taxis have, and that is that they will not carry any less than the number of people they can hold, so the green water taxi will only carry four people, not three people or two people or one person.

Students may find solutions such as six green water taxis, or four blue taxis and one green taxi. "*Now, what if there were 36 people who wanted to take water taxis to the shore; how many different ways could they load the green and blue water taxis?*"

NUMBER AND OPERATIONS: Developing an understanding of fractions and fraction equivalence

MATERIALS: Paper cutouts of apples, strips of paper measuring 12 inches long

In this story, Tad's grandma cooks a great big meal for his family. She loves to cook Polish foods like golumki, schmaltz, and wet pork chops. Does anyone know what golumkis are? How about schmaltz? Remember in the story how they describe these foods and other foods for the meal? Tad likes to help his grandma make the homemade applesauce; he enjoys peeling the apples and mashing them up to make the applesauce. His grandma wants him to make enough applesauce for the family of eight people, but he doesn't know how many apples he will need. Tad wants us to help him figure this out. His grandma's recipe calls for two apples to feed three people applesauce, so Tad needs us to help him figure out how many apples he should peel to make enough applesauce for eight people. His grandma tells him she does not want any applesauce leftover, so he is to make just enough for eight people. Let's work in our small groups to figure this out for Tad.

Students can work in small groups and use paper apples or draw various representations of apples being sorted into groups of two. The discussion can focus on the need to divide up the last two apples into thirds so Tad would see that he needs to peel 5 ⅓ apples to make enough applesauce for eight people. More problems could be created for Tad by changing the number of apples needed to make applesauce or change the number of people who will eat the applesauce.

In the tailor shop, Tad's uncle, Myron, makes the suits for the men who are hard to fit. He uses a measuring tape to measure the length of the men's legs, the width of their bellies, the length of their arms, and the length of their torso. Uncle Myron has a problem, though. He always loses his measuring tape, so he asked Tad if he could make him a new measuring tape in case he should lose the one he has. Tad wants us to try to make some measuring tapes that are 12 inches long and are marked in thirds, fourths, and halves. Can you show me with your hands how long you think 12 inches would be?

Another possibility here would be to have students mark off where they think 12 inches would be with a paper clip on a piece of string taped to the board.

Here is a strip of paper that measures 12 inches long. How do you think we could find out how to mark the inches on this strip of paper? Talk it over with your partner so we can get some ideas.

Give students the strips of paper and encourage them to think about how they could mark off the inches in the paper if they only know it measures 12 inches and they do not have any rulers. "*Now that we have inches on our paper strip, how can we add half inches?*" "*How can we mark quarter inches?*"

Now, let's use the measuring strips we just made to measure each other's pant lengths and arm lengths and put our measurements on this chart at the front board. Be sure to have two different people in your group do each measurement so we can compare the result to be sure the measures are accurate. We want to give these measurements to Uncle Myron so he can make suit coats that would fit us and not be too long or too short.

Extensions to this can have students create graphs with the various pant lengths and arm lengths to compare results. Also, differences can be discussed in measurements. If a student measured a pant length to be 10²/₄ inches, is that the same as 10½ inches? The students should be asked to prove they are the same.

GEOMETRY: Describing and analyzing properties of two-dimensional shapes

MATERIALS: Congruent triangle cutouts, pattern blocks

Tad's grandpa has some fabric in the shape of triangles left over from different suits that he made. He is wondering if he could put the triangles together to make some new shapes. What kind of shapes do you think he could make by putting some triangles together?

The teacher solicits some responses from the children. "*I have some triangles that are congruent. Talk to your partner and discuss what* congruent *means.*" The teacher gives students several minutes to discuss and then solicits responses to be sure they understand that congruent means the same shape and size.

Let's use these cutout triangles that are all congruent and see how many different shapes we can make. Grandpa wants to know how many different shapes we can find. Let's work in our groups to try to find some different shapes you can make with the triangles. Talk about the shapes in your group and write down some properties of the shapes that your group notices.

The teacher then gives students eight congruent triangles to use to explore the different shapes they can make.

Aunt Hattie loves to play the travel game with Tad. Did you notice how she fell asleep at the end of the story instead of Tad? Aunt Hattie likes to fall asleep after reading the story and playing the game, and she has always wanted a quilt to decorate her bed. She wants the quilt to look like some of the beautiful quilts that are made in Lancaster, Pennsylvania, a city she explored with Tad while playing the game. The Amish women make lots of hand-sewn quilts with different designs. So Aunt Hattie thought it would be great to have her own hand-sewn quilt made in the tailor shop. I know Grandpa has some square pieces of fabric, some triangles shapes, some hexagon shapes and some parallelogram fabric shapes that he cut out. Let's use our pattern blocks to model the pieces of fabric and create some beautiful designs that Grandpa could copy to make a quilt. Let's see if Grandpa could make a quilt by just using the squares. Then let's see if Grandpa could make a quilt by just using the hexagon pieces. What will Grandpa need to do if he wants to make a quilt using some of the parallelogram pieces?

This activity requires students to explore what shapes will fit together in a tessellation. The teacher engages students in thinking about which shapes fit together at each intersection and discusses the properties of the shapes. The concept of rotation and reflection can be introduced as students turn and flip the shapes to fit them into the tessellation.

Mathematical Curriculum Focal Points

TITLE AND AUTHOR OF BOOK:_____
_____
_____

AGE/GRADE OF CHILDREN: _____
_____
_____

NUMBER AND OPERATIONS
CURRICULUM FOCAL POINT:

PROBLEMS POSED:

MEASUREMENT
CURRICULUM FOCAL POINT:

PROBLEMS POSED:

GEOMETRY AND SPATIAL AWARENESS
CURRICULUM FOCAL POINT:

PROBLEMS POSED:

(continued)

PATTERNS AND RELATIONSHIPS
CURRICULUM FOCAL POINT:

PROBLEMS POSED:

DATA REPRESENTATION AND ANALYSIS
CURRICULUM FOCAL POINT:

PROBLEMS POSED:

NOTES:

_____

_____

_____

_____

_____

_____

_____

_____

_____

_____

_____

CHAPTER 8

Looking at Mathematics Beyond Storybooks: Informational Text

hildren are naturally curious about the world in which they live. Nonfiction or informational texts answer their curiosities and wonderment about their world. In fact, 60%–70% of elementary school libraries and children's sections of public libraries are books of nonfiction (Galda & Cullinan, 2002). Yet recent studies have indicated that children spend more time engaged with stories than with informational text. Duke (2000) found that an average of 3.6 minutes per day was spent with informational text in first-grade classrooms.

In many classrooms, informational texts are an integral part of the balanced literacy program. By definition, informational text is written to convey information about the world around us and contains specialized vocabulary toward that end (Purcell-Gates & Duke, 2001); thus informational texts build on children's inherent curiosities and inquiries about various topics, including science, animals, and the world. Informational texts are very well suited to supporting children's development of vocabulary and word knowledge. In fact, even before young children can read independently, there is growing evidence that they learn a great deal of vocabulary from texts read aloud to them (Elley, 1989; Dreher, 2000). Informational texts teach students new concepts and engage them in reading for understanding and reading for content. Pellegrini, Perlmutter, Galda, and Brody (1990) discovered that informational books that explain, define, and provide examples tend to elicit more joint participation and teaching opportunities in a shared book reading that provides readers with real-world information and specific vocabulary about people, places, events, and objects (Purcell-Gates & Duke, 2001). Nonfiction and informative texts make it possible to build background knowledge and vocabulary in ways that link the real world and children's interests with learning to read (Caswell & Duke, 1998). Thus teachers need to understand the developmental needs of young children to match their interests about topics with nonfiction books. When young children are interested in a topic, such as space, they are more likely to ask questions, learn new vocabulary, connect new knowledge to what they already know, and assimilate the information in the text.

In pre-K–3 classrooms, the integration of nonfiction literature can help teachers link children's reading skills to the learning of mathematical concepts. Reading materials such as *Weekly Reader* concept books, online web quests or web sites, and textbooks can set the stage for open-ended mathematical problems. Informational texts have many features designed to help readers navigate the material (McCall, 2003). When students learn about and begin to use these features, they can easily access information with clarity and comprehension. Teaching children about nonfiction features, the functions they serve, and how to recognize them will help them become successful readers of nonfiction. Three general categories of text features include 1) print features, 2) graphic aids, and 3) organizational aids (McCall, 2003).

Because informational texts can be used to help solve problems and answer questions and raise questions and pose problems, they can challenge readers to read critically while helping present familiar things in new and interesting ways. Informational books convey information, so teachers need to work with students to help them differentiate between nonfiction and fiction texts. Informational books can be used to pose mathematical thinking problems. Teachers can guide students to identify and analyze the mathematical information as they learn new facts. For example, a picture of a boat in an informational book such as *Boat Book* by Gail Gibbons (1983) could provide the context for a problem in which students wonder how far they think that boat could travel. Early childhood teachers could pose questions such as "How many people could fit into the boat?" Or "How many fish do they think could fit into the boat?" Questions for which there is no correct answer enable students to apply estimation and problem-solving strategies. More important, these types of problems require students to develop number sense, measurement sense, and estimation skills. The purpose of the activity is to engage students in critical thinking, reasoning, and mathematical discourse as students use materials and books from other disciplines.

When teachers surround children with compelling informational books, the visual components coupled with the expository language can extend the mathematical features to pose problems. In *Actual Size* (Jenkins, 2004), students can explore life-size images of animals or their body parts in their actual size and explore measurement and mathematical proportion such as ratio. In fact, Steven Jenkins (http://www.stevejenkinsbooks.com/) has published many nonfiction books for children, such as *Prehistoric Actual Size* (2005), *What Do You Do with a Tail Like This?* (2003), and *Down, Down, Down: A Journey to the Bottom of the Sea* (2008). All of the books help students explore animals, related attributes, measurement, and other mathematical concepts.

Reading across the disciplines can now also imply mathematics across the disciplines. Mathematics can be linked to content in informational texts in a way that makes it relevant and meaningful to all students. When content that is emphasized in the text is taught in a manner that connects to students' prior knowledge, teachers are able to assess the depth of their understanding and the need to focus on vocabulary, concepts, or skills. The integration of mathematical thinking along with the content in the text creates opportunities for children to think about the content from a real-world or imaginary approach. In the example that follows, the book on whales introduces facts and vocabulary about whales to children. The content is presented as information to learn. However, when the teacher has the children pretend that the whales are swimming into a bay in pairs, or that a whale has landed on the beach and they have to figure out how to measure it, all of a sudden the whales appear real and the students' attention and imagination are engaged. The informational text content has stimulated their intellect and engaged them in mathematical problem solving and explorations. According to research, children learn through narrative or story form better than through expository instruction (Seifert, 1993). Not only are the children learning mathematical strategies and problem solving but also they are learning the content of the text.

NCTM strongly encourages the connection between mathematics and other disciplines. As stated in the *Principles and Standards for School Mathematics*, "When students connect mathematical ideas, their understanding is deeper and more lasting" (NCTM, 2000, p. 64). They begin to see mathematics as a whole rather than as a collection of separate strands. Integrating mathematics with other content areas also helps teachers meet the ever-growing need to address greater amounts of information in the curriculum. As students link concepts in informational texts with mathematics and apply mathematical thinking, they begin to see that there are no boundaries to what they learn. They also see how the process of solving problems can be applied to contexts outside of mathematics. Thus it is important for teachers to continually create these problem-solving opportunities and learn to pose open-ended problems around the texts.

Let's look at some mathematics problems from a second-grade classroom based on a book about whales.

LESSON PLAN: Second-Grade Example

BOOK: Gibbons, G. (1991). *Whales.* New York: Holiday House. (Illustration copyright © 1991 by Gail Gibbons. All rights reserved. Reprinted by permission of Holiday House, Inc.)

SECOND-GRADE CURRICULUM FOCAL POINTS: Develop quick recall of addition and related subtraction facts. Develop an understanding of linear measurement and facility with measuring lengths.

MATERIALS: Counters, string

So, why do you think the whales swam into the bay? I know the book only spoke about 2 whales that swam into the bay, but what if there were 10 whales that swam into the bay in pairs? Let's count by twos up to 10. What if there were 20 whales in the bay? Can we count by twos up to 20? (Students count by twos to 20 with the teacher pointing to the numbers on the hundreds chart.) Let's say the whales are swimming into the bay in a pattern. First, one whale enters, then two whales enter, then three whales enter, then four whales enter the bay. If this pattern continues, how many whales would enter the bay next?

The students respond with "5."

Can you use the counters on your tables to model the pattern that the whales are following? Take a few minutes to show the pattern the whales are using to swim.

Great! Now in the book they showed a picture of a whale on the beach that washed ashore. The people along the beach needed to call the marine rescue squad to let them know a whale was on the beach. The rescue squad dispatcher asked them how long the whale was. How do you think they could measure a whale?

The teacher solicits creative responses from the students. *"Can we estimate how long you think a whale might be? How long do you think the whale is? Let's put our estimates on the board."* Students give their estimates. The teacher says, *"I have a string that I cut that is the length of an average-sized whale."* The teacher holds up the string. *"Let's lay the string on the ground and look at how long a whale can be. Then each of you can walk along the length of the string and count how many steps long the whale measures."* The teacher lays the string on the ground and the students walk along the length of the string. *"Can you think of something in the school that would be the same length as the whale? Let's see if the whale is bigger than our classroom door."* The teacher holds up the string to compare the length of the door and the length of the whale. The lesson can continue comparing other objects in the classroom or school.

Let's look at another second-grade mathematics class and the problems the teacher posed around the children's book *The Great Kapok Tree: A Tale of the Amazon Rain Forest* (Cherry, 1990) at the beginning of the school year.

LESSON PLAN: Second-Grade Example

BOOK: Cherry, L. (1990). *The great kapok tree: A tale of the Amazon rain forest.* New York: Scholastic.

SYNOPSIS: The story explains the ecological importance of saving the rainforests. Several inhabitants from the forest sneak up on a man who fell asleep as he started to cut down the kapok tree. They whisper reasons why he should not cut down the tree in his ear. When he awakens, he looks around and realizes the beauty and harmony of all the living things in the forest.

SECOND-GRADE CURRICULUM FOCAL POINT: Developing an understanding of the base 10 numeration system and place-value concepts

MATERIALS: Whiteboards, base 10 blocks, hundred charts

After having read the book earlier in a reading circle, the teacher guided the children to look at the beautiful illustrations in the book and at a picture of the large kapok tree. *"Let's look at this picture of the kapok tree. Do you think it would be easy to count all the branches on the tree? Why do you think that?"* The teacher solicits responses from the students.

I think most of you can see how tricky it is to count all the branches because the picture might not show them all. I wonder how many branches are on the tree? Do you think you could write an estimate of the number of branches you think the tree has on your whiteboards? Let's take a minute and look at the picture and write an estimate for the number of branches the tree might have. Great! Everyone has an estimate written. Can someone share with us what it means when we estimate?

The teacher solicits a response from a student who tells the class that an estimate is a good guess.

Does everyone agree that an estimate is a good guess? Very good! Now, what I would like you to do is to bring your whiteboards to the front of the room and arrange yourselves in order from the lowest estimate to the greatest estimate.

The children take time to arrange themselves in order with little help from the teacher. *"Nicely done! Now, let's look at what are the lowest and the greatest estimates. Let's have the children who made the lowest and greatest estimates take a few steps forward."* The children identify the two estimates.

Okay, what I would like everyone to do is look at the lowest and greatest estimates and think about how you could find the difference between them. Let's go back to our groups and work on finding the difference between the estimates. You have base 10 blocks at your tables to use if you need them.

Because the children had not yet learned any algorithms for subtracting double-digit numbers, the teacher was looking for some invented strategies or reasoning with number sense. Once the groups had time to work on the problem, the teacher asked them to share their strategies for finding a solution with the class. She later introduced the term *range* and defined it as the difference between the greatest and lowest estimate. She wrote the word on a piece of cardstock and hung it on the bulletin board to refer to again later in the curriculum.

Later, the teacher returned to the book.

Let's look at the book again. Do you see this monkey on this page? The monkey whispered in my ear and told me he counted 34 branches on the kapok tree. Pretend the monkey is sitting on a chair next to me, and the monkey wants to know what 34 looks like. Can you use your base 10 blocks to show the monkey a way to represent 34? Let's take a minute to show the monkey how to represent 34.

After the children pair-shared their solutions, the teacher asked the children to represent the number in a different way, encouraging them to see that they could use 2 tens and 14 ones, 1 ten and 24 ones, or 34 ones. Her goal was to have the children represent numbers in multiple ways and use problem-solving strategies to find the difference in the number of branches estimated. The children were excited to explain how they found the difference in the number of branches estimated, with some using the hundreds chart and others using base 10 blocks.

Posing problems based on the context of this book helped the children make meaningful and relevant connections to the mathematics. In this example, children were learning about the kapok tree and the South American area at the same time they were enthusiastically engaged in trying to find the difference between the estimates. The open-ended problems the teacher posed required the children to think critically and explore mathematical approaches to finding the difference between two multidigit numbers. They were problems that could have been presented without the storybook context by just presenting two numbers and having the children discover an algorithm to find the difference. However, the storybook gave the problems some meaning and made them relevant to the children. They were excited to solve the problems and describe their strategies.

Informational texts convey important information for children to learn. By providing children with these rich experiences to connect the mathematics with the content, they will begin to use more advanced modes of reasoning (Althouse, 1994). Their knowledge and language skills will also increase with the focus on the content of the text. As teachers embed problem-solving activities within informational texts, they see how this process provides opportunities for students to "contextualize mathematics in a situation that will catch their attention, stir their interest, arouse their feelings, stimulate their intellect, and propel them to actively engage with the mathematics" (Schiro, 2004, p. 63).

# References

Althouse, R. (1994). *Investigating mathematics with young children*. New York: Teachers College Press.

Anderson, L.W., & Krathwohl, D.R. (Eds.). (2001). *A taxonomy for learning, teaching and assessing: A revision of Bloom's Taxonomy of educational objectives*. New York: Longman.

Banks, J.A. (1994). *Multi-ethnic education: Theory and practice*. Needham Heights, MA: Allyn & Bacon.

Carlson, A.D. (1996). Concept books and young children. In K. Vandergrift (Ed.), *Ways of knowing: Literature and the intellectual life of children* (pp. 185–202). Lanham, MD: Scarecrow Press.

Caswell, L.J., & Duke, N.K. (1998). Non-narrative as a catalyst for literacy development. *Language Arts, 75*(2), 108–117.

Copley, J. (Ed.). (2000). *Mathematics in the early years, birth to five*. Reston, VA: National Council of Teachers of Mathematics.

Copley, J.V. (2000). *The young child and mathematics*. Washington, DC: National Association for the Education of Young Children.

Copple, C., & Bredekamp, S. (2009). *Developmentally appropriate practice in early childhood programs serving children from birth through age 8*. Washington, DC: National Association for the Education of Young Children.

Darling-Hammond, L. (1996). The right to learn and the advancement of teaching: Research, policy, and practice for democratic education. *Educational Researcher, 25*(6), 5–17.

Dreher, M.J. (2000). Fostering reading for learning. In L. Baker, M.J. Dreher, & J. Guthrie (Eds.), *Engaging young readers: Promoting achievement and motivation* (pp. 94–118). New York: Guilford.

Duke, N.K. (2000). 3.6 minutes per day: The scarcity of informational text in first grade. *Reading Research Quarterly, 35*(1), 202–224.

Edwards, E. (Ed.). (1980). *The agenda for action*. Reston, VA: National Council of Teachers of Mathematics.

Egan, K. (2005). *An imaginative approach to teaching*. San Francisco: Jossey-Bass.

Elley, W.B. (1989). Vocabulary acquisition from listening to stories. *Reading Research Quarterly, 24*(2), 174–187.

Friedman, T. (2005). *The world is flat: A brief history of the twenty-first century*. New York: Farrar, Straus & Giroux.

Galda, L., & Cullinan, B.E. (2002). *Literature and the child*. Belmont: Wadsworth/Thomson Learning.

Ginsburg, H.P., Inoue, N., & Seo, K. (1999). Young children doing mathematics: Observation of everyday activities. In J.V. Copley (Ed.), *Mathematics in the early years*. Reston, VA: National Council of Teachers of Mathematics.

Giorgis, C., & Glazer, J. (2009). *Literature for young children: Supporting emergent literacy, ages 0–8* (6th ed.). New York: Allyn & Bacon.

Good, T.L., & Brophy, J.E. (1987). *Looking in classroom*. New York: Harper & Row.

Hong, H. (1996). Effects of mathematics learning through children's literature on math achievement and dispositional outcomes. *Early Childhood Research Quarterly, 11*, 477–494.

Howes, C. (2003). *Teaching 4- to 8-year-olds: Literacy, math, multiculturalism, and class-room community*. Baltimore: Paul H. Brookes Publishing Co.

Hunsader, P.D. (2004). Mathematics trade books: Establishing their value and assessing their quality. *The Reading Teacher 57*(7), 618–629.

Hyson, M. (2008). *Enthusiastic and engaged learners: Approaches to learning in the early childhood classroom*. New York: Teachers College Press.

Jalongo, M.R. (2004). *Young children and picture books* (2nd ed.). Washington, DC: National Association for the Education of Young Children.

Krasa, N., & Shunkwiler, S. (2009). *Number sense and number nonsense: Understanding the challenges of learning math*. Baltimore: Paul H. Brookes Publishing Co.

McCall, J. (2003). Using text features as tools for learning. In L. Hoyt, M. Mooney, & B. Parkes (Eds.), *Exploring informational texts: From theory to practice* (pp. 50–51). Portsmouth, NH: Heinemann.

Morrow, L.M. (1985). Retelling stories: A strategy for improving young children's comprehension, concept of story structure, and oral language complexity. *The Elementary School Journal, 85*(5), 646–661.

Morrow, L.M., Freitag, E., & Gambrell, L.B. (2009). *Using children's literature in preschool to develop comprehension: Understanding and enjoying books*. Newark, NJ: International Reading Association.

National Association for the Education of Young Children & National Council of Teachers of Mathematics. (2002). *Early childhood education: Promoting good beginnings*. Washington, DC: Author.

National Council for the Social Studies. (1997). *National standards for social studies teachers*. Washington, DC: Author.

National Council of Teachers of Mathematics. (2000). *Principles and standards for school mathematics*. Reston, VA: Author.

National Council of Teachers of Mathematics. (2006). *Curriculum focal points for pre-kindergarten through grade 8 mathematics: A quest for coherence*. Reston, VA: Author.

Pellegrini, A.D., Perlmutter, J.C., Galda, L., & Brody, G.H. (1990). Joint reading between black Head Start children and their mothers. *Child Development, 61*(2), 443–453.

Pressley, M., & Hilden, K. (2002). How can children be taught to comprehend text better? In M.L. Kamil, J.B. Manning, & H.J. Walberg (Eds.), *Successful reading instruction* (pp. 33–53). Greenwich, CT: Information Age.

Purcell-Gates, V., & Duke, N.K. (2001, August). *Explicit explanation/teaching of informational text genres: A model for research*. Paper presented at the National Science Foundation Conference, "Crossing Borders: Connection Science and Literacy," Baltimore.

Schiro, M.S. (1997). *Integrating children's literature and mathematics in the classroom: Children as meaning makers, problem solvers, and literary critics*. New York: Teachers College Press.

Schiro, M.S. (2004). *Oral storytelling and teaching mathematics: Pedagogical and multicultural perspectives*. Thousand Oaks, CA: Sage Publications.

Seifert, K.L. (1993). Cognitive development and early childhood education. In B. Spodek (Ed.), *Handbook of research on the education of young children* (pp. 10–15). New York: Macmillan.

Sophian, C. (1999). Children's ways of knowing: Lessons from cognitive development research. In J. Copley (Ed.), *Mathematics in the early years*. Reston, VA: National Council of Teachers of Mathematics.

Turner, L.A., & Johnson, B. (2003). A model of mastery motivation for at-risk preschoolers. *Journal of Educational Psychology, 95*(3), 495–505.

Vygotsky, L. (1978). *Mind in society*. Cambridge: Harvard University Press.

Wilburne, J., Napoli, M., Keat, J., Dile, K., Trout, M., & Decker, S. (2007). Journeying into mathematics through storybooks: A kindergarten study. *Teaching Children's Mathematics, 14*(4), 232–237.

Children's Books

Aardema, V. (1992). *Bringing the rain to Kapiti plain.* New York: Penguin Group.

Allen, P. (1996). *Who sank the boat?* New York: Putnam Publishing Group.

Auch, M. (2002). *The princess and the pizza.* New York: Holiday House.

Brisson, P. (1995). *Benny's pennies.* New York: Bantam Doubleday Books for Young Readers.

Bryan, A. (2003). *Beautiful blackbird.* New York: Atheneum Books for Young Readers.

Capucilli, K. (2001). *The jelly bean fun book.* New York: Little Simon.

Chamberlin, M., & Chamberlin, R. (2005). *Mama Panya's pancakes: A village tale from Kenya.* Cambridge, MA: Barefoot Books.

Chen, C.Y. (2004). *Guji Guji.* La Jolla, CA: Kane/Miller Book Publishers.

Cherry, L. (1990). *The great kapok tree: A tale of the Amazon rain forest.* New York: Scholastic.

Dodds, D.A. (2004). *Minnie's diner: A multiplying menu.* Somerville, MA: Candlewick Press.

Feiffer, J. (1999). *Meanwhile.* New York: HarperCollins Publishing.

Flournoy, V. (1985). *The patchwork quilt.* New York: Dial Books for Young Readers.

French, J. (2003). *Diary of a wombat.* New York: Clarion Books.

Friedman, A. (1994). *A cloak for the dreamer.* New York: Scholastic.

Gibbons, G. (1983). *Boat book.* New York: Holiday House.

Gibbons, G. (1991). *Whales.* New York: Holiday House.

Grandits, J. (2009). *The travel game.* New York: Clarion Books.

Hest, A. (2009). *Little chick.* Somerville, MA: Candlewick Press.

Hutchins, P. (1986). *The doorbell rang.* New York: Greenwillow.

Jenkins, S. (2004). *Actual size.* Boston: Houghton Mifflin.

Jenkins, S. (2005). *Prehistoric actual size.* Boston: Houghton Mifflin.

Jenkins, S. (2008). *Down, down, down: A journey to the bottom of the sea.* Boston: Houghton Mifflin Harcourt.

Jenkins, S., & Page, R. (2003). *What do you do with a tail like this?* Boston: Houghton Mifflin.

Kitamura, S. (1986). *When sheep cannot sleep: The counting book.* New York: Farrar, Straus & Giroux.

Krensky, S. (2009). *Chaucer's first winter.* New York: Simon & Schuster Books for Young Readers.

Lionni, L. (1973). *Swimmy.* New York: Random House.

Merriam, E. (1993). *12 ways to get to 11.* New York: Simon & Schuster Books for Young Readers.

Moore, I. (1991). *Six-Dinner Sid.* New York: Simon & Schuster Children's Books.

Morrow, B.O. (2009). *Mr. Mosquito puts on his tuxedo.* New York: Holiday House.

Moss, L. (2001). *Our marching band.* New York: G.P. Putnam's Sons.

Piper, W. (1976). *The little engine that could.* New York: Penguin Putnam Books for Young Readers.

Pittman, H.C. (1986). *A grain of rice.* New York: Yearling.

Plourde, L. (2007). *A mountain of mittens.* Watertown, MA: Charlesbridge.

Rodriquez, E. (2008). *Sergio makes a splash.* New York: Little, Brown Books for Young Readers.

Sams, C.R. II, & Stoick, J. (2004). *Lost in the woods: A photographic fantasy.* Milford, MI: Carl R. Sams II Photography.

Tierney, F. (2010). *Lion's lunch?* New York: Chicken House.

Van Allsburg, C. (1990). *Just a dream.* Boston: Houghton Mifflin.

Viorst, J. (1972). *Alexander and the terrible, horrible, no good, very bad day.* New York: Atheneum Books for Young Readers.

Waddell, M. (1992). *Owl babies.* Cambridge, MA: Candlewick Press.

Williams, R.L. (2001). *The coin counting book.* Watertown, MA: Charlesbridge.

Williams, V.B. (1982). *A chair for my mother.* New York: Scholastic.

Winnick, K.B. (2004). *The night of the fireflies.* Honesdale, PA: Boyds Mill Press.

Wood, A. (1984). *The napping house.* San Diego: Harcourt Brace.

Zemach, K. (2003). *Just enough.* New York: Scholastic Press.

Web Resources to Access High-Quality Storybooks for the Classroom

The following links provide information about high-quality storybooks to use in the classroom to link literacy and mathematical thinking. Please note that the resources are listed alphabetically.

The American Library Association
http://www.ala.org
Every year, the American Library Association honors illustrators and authors with numerous awards including the Caldecott award, Coretta Scott King Award, Pura Belpré award, Robert Siebert award, and others.

Bank Street College Best Book list
http://www.bankstreet.edu/childrenslibrary/booklists
The list of books is compiled by an expert panel to identify how books can affect young readers, and what books can do for them.

Book Links
https://cs.ala.org/booklinks/search.cfm
Book Links features themed articles pertaining to children's books to curriculum areas such as math, social studies, and so forth. There is a searchable cumulative index and selected articles from issues since 1999.

BookHive
http://www.plcmc.org/bookhive/
This web site is designed for children ages birth through 12 years and their parents, teachers, and anyone else who is interested in reading about children's books. The site contains hundreds of recommended book reviews across a variety of reading levels and interest areas.

Booklist
http://www.booklistonline.com/
This is an electronic companion to the print version and includes a searchable index, feature articles, book reviews, and so forth and is sponsored by the American Library Association.

Bulletin of Center for Children's Books
http://bccb.lis.illinois.edu/
This is a reputable book review journal sponsored by the University of Illinois with an accompanying web page with searchable database for subscribers.

The Children's Book Council
http://www.cbcbooks.org/
The Children's Book Council is the national nonprofit trade association for children's trade book publishers. This web site is full of wonderful resources, including lists of books and new releases for building library collections.

Children's Choices Award
http://www.reading.org/resources/booklists/childrenschoices.aspx
This book list is the result of a cosponsored project of the International Reading Association and the Children's Book Council, which features children's choices of their favorite books. The complete annotated Children's Choices list appears each year in the October issue of *The Reading Teacher*.

Children's Literature Assembly
http://www.childrensliteratureassembly.org/index.htm
The Children's Literature Assembly of the National Council of Teachers of English (http://www.ncte.org) advocates the importance of utilizing literature for teaching children and young adults. Information about the Notable Books for Language Arts can be found on their web site.

The Children's Literature Web Guide
http://www.acs.ucalgary.ca/~dkbrown/index.html
This site provides readers with extensive Internet resources related to children's literature, including discussion groups, classroom activities, and information related to children's literature.

The Five Owls
http://www.fiveowls.com/
A quarterly publication that presents book reviews and articles about books and reading.

Horn Book
http://www.hbook.com/
For more than 75 years, the Horn Book has provided book reviews, articles, and editorials. In addition, it provides information about the Boston Globe Horn Book Awards. There is also a blog and online newsletter that features interviews and reviews.

Interesting Nonfiction for Kids (I.N.K.)
http://www.inkrethink.blogspot.com
I.N.K. is a web site with many postings by notable nonfiction writers and includes lists of books for the classroom.

International Board on Books for Young People
http://www.ibby.org/index.html
International Board on Books for Young People (IBBY) is an international non-profit organization whose goal is to connect books and children. IBBY awards the Hans Christian Andersen Awards every other year. Besides sponsoring International Children's Book Day, the organization hold seminars, workshops, and congresses.

International Children's Digital Library Foundation
http://en.childrenslibrary.org/
The International Children's Digital Library Foundation provides a digital library of outstanding children's books from around the world.

Jim Trelease, The Read-Aloud Handbook
http://www.trelease-on-reading.com/
This informative web site includes a searchable database of recommended titles to share with children as well as other resources advocating the benefits of reading aloud.

Kirkus (Children's) Reviews
http://www.kirkusreviews.com/
This site provides both online and print information about prepublication reviews. Founded in 1933, this service includes sections: fiction, mysteries, science fiction, foreign languages, and nonfiction.

Literature for Science and Mathematics:
Kindergarten Through Grade Twelve
http://www.cde.ca.gov/ci/sc/ll/
This web site is a searchable collection of outstanding science- and mathematics-related literature for children and adolescents. The recommended titles reflect the quality and the complexity of the types of materials students should be reading at school and outside of class.

Living Math
http://www.livingmath.net/Home/tabid/250/language/en-US/Default.aspx
Living Math is a site with articles and book lists for teachers who want to integrate literature and math within the classroom.

Mathematical Fiction
http://kasmana.people.cofc.edu/MATHFICT/
This web site is a searchable database for teachers to locate children's books to align with math concepts.

Math Solutions/Marilyn Burns
http://www.mathsolutions.com/
This web site features book lists compiled by Marilyn Burns to improve the learning and teaching of mathematics in schools.

Nancy Keane Book Talks
http://www.nancykeane.com/booktalks/
This is a rich site that provides bibliographies and annotated bibliographies of children's books. Books are categorized by author, subject, title, and grade level. Also included are recommended reading lists, book review sources, and tips on giving book talks.

The Notable Books for a Global Society
http://www.tcnj.edu/~childlit/
The NBGS award is selected by a committee of the International Reading Association Children's Literature and Reading Special Interest Group. The committee selects a list of outstanding trade books for enhancing student understanding of people and cultures throughout the world. Winning titles include fiction, nonfic-

tion, and poetry written for students in Grades K–12. The winning titles each year are announced at the International Reading Association Convention. An article describing the selections is included in the *The Dragon Lode*.

Orbis Pictus Award
http://www.ncte.org/awards/orbispictus
The Orbis Pictus Award recognizes excellence in the writing of nonfiction for children and young adults and is sponsored by the National Council of Teachers of English (www.ncte.org).

Pennsylvania Center for the Book
http://pabook.libraries.psu.edu/
The Pennsylvania Center for the Book works with hundreds of children's books each year while preparing booklists, activities, and curriculum materials. The Family Literacy Activities web page is designed to help parents and caregivers fill each child's world with a love of books. The Baker's Dozen list includes the very best picture books published for young children with activities to promote family literacy.

Publisher's Weekly
http://www.publishersweekly.com/pw/home/index.html
Publisher's Weekly serves those involved in creating, producing, and selling written work in audio, video, and electronic formats, as well as print. Web extras include numerous current and archived articles, lists, newsletters, and a searchable index.

School Library Journal
http://www.schoollibraryjournal.com/
This is an extensive publication that features reviews of all media. There is also a database with book talks, audio of the week, and much more.

The Spaghetti Book Club
http://www.spaghettibookclub.org/
The Spaghetti Book Club web site is a place for kids who love to read and talk about books. It is a very good site for students to read reviews and to post their own thoughts about books that they have read.

Worlds of Words
http://www.wowlit.org
This web site provides an online database of global children's and adolescent literature, searchable by theme, age, country, and more.

Index

Tables and figures are indicated by *t* and *f*, respectively.